Warren, Rhode Island

YANKEE MAGAZINE'S

New England:

Special Places & Certain People

Nelson, New Hampshire

YANKEE MAGAZINE'S
New England:
Special Places & Certain People

A Selection of the Best and Most Beautiful of
Yankee's "This New England" series.

Edited by Edie Clark

A division of Yankee Publishing Incorporated
Dublin, New Hampshire

Designer and Picture Editor: **J Porter**
Assistant Designer and Picture Editor: **Andrea N. Meagher**
Picture Research: **Jamie Kageleiry**

Yankee Publishing Incorporated
Dublin, New Hampshire 03444

Library of Congress Catalog Card Number: 86-50092
ISBN: 0-89909-104-0

Contents

Squam Lakes, New Hampshire

Acknowledgements

Granville, Vermont

IT ISN'T THAT EASY TO SAY JUST WHAT IT IS THAT MAKES A town or a place special enough to make it one of the features in our "This New England" series. Towns are like people — some are more interesting than others: they may have an interesting background, they might be extraordinarily beautiful, or they may have worked their way through a particularly difficult trial. Whatever aspect it is that sets these towns apart, this is what we look for when we go out on the road, crisscrossing New England, looking for parts of this region that in some way exemplify the whole — a whole that is exceptionally complex.

Almost without exception, the people of these towns have welcomed us into their homes and given us the warmth of their hospitality. In so many cases, that well-known New England quality of taciturnity seems to vanish, and people have shown us their towns in a way we never could have known them on our own. To all the people of these towns, far too numerous to list, our thanks.

Thanks also to those who shared in the preparation of this book: Jud Hale, Dick Heckman, Sharon Smith, John Pierce, Ben Watson, Nancy Fuchs, Mary Werner, and special thanks to Paul Bolton.

– Edie Clark

Introduction

Glover, Vermont

THOSE OF US WHO CHOOSE TO LIVE IN NEW ENGLAND clearly understand the importance of such things as boundaries, but we also have a certain feeling for the region. This intuitive sense of what defines New England often causes us to speak of the scale of the landscape, trying to describe how hillside farms in Vermont and western New Hampshire just plain fit into the land. We might also mention Connecticut towns with handsome town greens surrounded by four-square Colonial houses. "Just like the movies," an occasional visitor is heard to murmur at appropriate vistas. Of course, Hollywood had to get the idea somewhere.

New England has long been an enviable source of scenic images to which people respond. When *Yankee* Magazine's editor and co-founder Robb Sagendorph started the "This New England" series in the September 1955 issue, the announcement was simple enough: "This month *Yankee* begins a new series of photographic essays on New England villages and towns." The birth of the series was a reaction to the readers' expressed interest in actually seeing what life was like around the six-state region. The idea struck a nerve. From that little sentence has sprung a department that is part of the backbone of each issue of the magazine. The story and photographs about a unique location each month give the readers a sense of place.

This feeling of being somewhere is what we try to convey when we describe our home, our hometown, or our region. This is why the series has meant so much to *Yankee* readers over the years. The writers and photographers who bring locations alive each month are all trying to capture the feeling someone would have if he or she lived in that particular place.

The process of finding and reporting on a particular place each month is an interesting challenge. Some communities have a sense of place that can be captured with ease. Others remain elusive, sometimes forever. A town like Wilsons Mills, Maine, where the townspeople appropriate money to feed the local deer every winter, is a story just waiting to be told. One has an immediate sense of something that makes life there unique. Other towns, like Middletown Springs, Vermont, have been so shaped by their geography and their history that the past remains a powerful presence in the here and now. Understanding that connection makes the readers feel they know the town. Sometimes, as is the case with Richmond, Maine, the people in a community — there, Russian immigrants — are the fabric of the story. Their lives, their history help delineate their town. What is most often the truth, however, is that pieces of all of these elements combine to create a clear and memorable image of a community.

In recent years, we have deviated a bit from the original charter, but are confident that Mr. Sagendorph would approve. We now show more than just towns and villages. Lakes and rivers are unique settings, and life along them or around them is shaped by the body of water. Neighborhoods in cities, or even whole cities themselves, are also recorded here for your enjoyment. They, too, offer a special sense of place in a vital and less pastoral way. All of these themes have appeared in "This New England" and will continue to appear in issues to come, along with new ideas yet to be conceived.

So please take this opportunity to visit different corners of the region that enjoys the shared perception of somehow being "America's hometown." So many of the values that people associate with small-town life seem to have their origins here in New England. Those of us who live here are proud to be the temporary keepers of such treasures. Without them we would not feel at home here. We would not have that essential sense of who we are and where we are. We would be without that sense of place.

– John Pierce
Managing Editor
Yankee *Magazine*

Middletown Springs, Vermont

by Edie Clark • Photographs by Richard W. Brown

MIDDLETOWN SPRINGS sits in a valley with hills growing up all around. The town center is easy to miss as you pass through this west side of Vermont, wild with a roller coaster of hills, where cows and sheep graze on ledges they've etched into the hillsides like stripes on a barber pole. But if you stop and look, you'll see fine Victorian homes, unusually ornate and lavish. These homes are all that is left to remind us of the wealth that came into this town all at once, when, at the end of the last century, water meant gold to Middletown Springs.

Up until 1885 the town was called Middletown, named for the hometown of one of the settlers from Connecticut. What with war, floods, and a disastrous flu epidemic, things had been touch and go for this small farming village located south of Rutland, near the New York border. In 1791 the population was 699, and although today it barely reaches 600, in between there was the discovery of the springs and all that those waters could supposedly do for a newly urbanized nation, desperate for what their new money could not buy: good health.

Alice Gray Hickox is the great-granddaughter of A. W. Gray, the force behind the spa that mushroomed in the center of Middletown, the spa that changed the town's name and the nature of its reputation. Miss Hickox is a very alert 94, and she lives in a house not far from the springs, the same

A.W. Gray (above) saw a great future in the springs that bubbled up a rather bitter mineral water. To make the spa appear more elegant to New Yorkers, later brochures showed a dining room that looked like it was at least a quarter of a mile long (below).

house that A. W. built for himself and his family in 1851. Though she was only a very young girl, she remembers when the town would swell in the summer with wealthy out-of-town visitors who would arrive by train in Poultney and then come into Middletown on the stagecoach that rattled into town twice a day. According to her family's lore, the Indians tipped off the early settlers that the springs had healing powers. "They thought that since the waters tasted bitter, they must be good for them," Miss Hickox explains. Her great-grandfather was an innovative man who invented the thresher and the "horse-power machine" (treadmill), and it was he who perceived the springs' hidden potential and capitalized on them, building first the spring-house and the bottling plant and then, shortly, the large luxury hotel up on Barber Mountain. "But," Miss Hickox adds, tongue in cheek, "I don't know just how healthful the water really was."

There are three springs in the fork where the Poultney and North rivers join. The bottling plant was at that fork where now there are only ferns and watercress. Nearby are the stone abutments that supported the footbridge that led to the Montvert Hotel, once described as "one of the most charming and healthful summer resorts in America." But the public's fascination with summer "watering places" was

Once one of the lavish homes in town, this is now Middletown Springs Inn.

14

Believers in the water's powers could buy in bottles (top), *which also came in blue and green, or sample at the springhouse* (above), *which was destroyed in a 1927 flood but rebuilt in detail* (right) *by the Historical Society.*

short-lived; the hotel was torn down in 1906, its lumber sold to local house builders.

With no ocean or majestic mountain to sustain its potential as a resort, Middletown Springs went back to counting on cows and sheep to keep it going, and for a while the only thing to remind the town of the dazzling mo-

ment in its history was the bottles.

The old brown bottles, with "Middletown Healing Springs/Gray & Clark/Middletown, Vermont" pressed in an oval logo on the face, are collectibles to townspeople. They are hard to find, and as Alice Hickox rightly observes, no one can be collecting them very fast. She keeps the one that she

has, passed down from A. W., in her china closet in the dining room, and she and her brother-in-law, Herb Davison, who is the town's historian, try to keep track of who else in town has one. Or more than one.

Paul and Anna Fenton, who live on a dairy farm on Spruce Knob Road, have one that's been made into a lamp, one

in the cellar that's got wine in it, and one saved up for each of their grandchildren. The Fentons also try to keep track of who in town has one of the bottles, which also came in blue or green. Last year they had their family clock repaired, and Anna says that all the man wanted in payment was a spring bottle.

Anna, who wears her gray hair tied in a knot at the back of her head, is a big, comfortable woman whose eyes suggest strength. She has lived all of her 80 years on this farm, which belonged to her grandfather and to her grandmother, who Anna says was healed by the Middletown waters. In an overfull closet Anna keeps a packet of photographs,

sales brochures, and dinner menus from the Montvert. The pictures show a grand hotel, more appropriate to the Jersey shore, with four stories and lines of dormer windows that looked out over the hills. There was a marble fountain out front and a wide porch all around, and for those not too infirm when they got there, there was lawn

Anna and Paul Fenton keep track of who in town has one of the bottles.

tennis and croquet and a bowling alley. There was room for 250 guests, who paid $1.50 a night for a room and all their meals. Guests came from New York City or from Boston or even from Baltimore to the spa that once rivaled Saratoga Springs. They came for the cure, but the sales brochure, with its pictures of ladies with parasols and men in straw boaters, suggested a holiday instead.

Herb Davison, whose sharp eyes be-

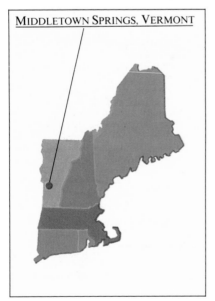

MIDDLETOWN SPRINGS, VERMONT

hind round rimless glasses seem to miss no detail, has gone to some effort to record Middletown Springs' history accurately. According to Herb, the hotel flourished under the direction of A. W. and his sons, but shortly after A. W. died, the hotel was sold to a group of New Yorkers headed by Jacob Eager. Mr. Eager put out a new brochure, a copy of which Herb keeps on display at the historical society. He enjoys a good chuckle over the liberties which the New Yorkers took in advertising their Vermont property. Though the Mont-vert really did have elegance and grace, Herb says that the drawings on the cover of the newer brochure added a full story to the hotel's height and many extra windows along each side, and added ten or so feet to the gushing geyser of the marble fountain out front. Inside, the copy claimed that the hotel was "3,000 feet above sea level, which

places it above the malarial line, where mosquitoes do not exist . . ." In fact, Herb Davison points out, the town's elevation is only 960 feet, and they've got mosquitoes just like everyone else. "The drawings in the old brochures did exaggerate the elegance of the Mont-vert," Herb says. "They've got a drawing of a dining room in here that looks like it's big enough for the 220-yard dash, but it was really just an ordinary room. I am sure," he adds, "that the hyperboles were not caused by drinking the mineral springs water!"

Hyperboles and truth in advertising aside, the people who came believed in the possibilities, and when they left they packed away in their suitcases a supply of the waters in stout glass bottles with labels that boasted cures for every ailment imaginable — from hangnails or hay fever to cancer, malaria, or syphilis.

Over the years, the town had almost forgotten about the hotel and the springs and the lore that went with them. But an influx of newcomers brought renewed interest in this town's story. Until 1971 the springs lay buried under several feet of river silt, washed over by time and flooding. A committee of 70 local people, among them Herb Davison, got together and dug down to the old marble thresholds, and all three of the springs flowed once again. The group also studied old photographs, drew up plans, and rebuilt the springhouse in painstaking detail.

This October Middletown Springs will celebrate its bicentennial. Though the town remains small, its people speak of it as if they'd take on the world in its cause. There are those, like Alice Hickox and the Fentons, whose roots reach back nearly to the town's beginnings. And there are newcomers who

have come, like the visitors to the spa once did, from New Jersey and Baltimore and Boston, and settled into life there with all the fervor of lifelong residents. Jim and Janet Webber came to Middletown Springs eight years ago from New Jersey and set up an antiques shop. As Herb Davison can tell you, not long after they moved there, the Webbers bought one of the old bottles, one with a paper label, at an auction in New York and brought it home to Middletown Springs, where they show it off with pride. They urge family and old friends from down-country to come visit, and when they do, Janet takes them on a tour like an old-timer. She drives up Coy Hill to the Semans' place, from whose garden you can look down into the village. From there, she goes up over the ridge to show off the view from Ellen and John Moyer's dairy farm, which overlooks a platoon

of rounded hills, an outlook that Ellen says lets her see the snow coming and the lightning, too. Then Janet drives over to Burnham Hollow Orchards, which in the spring, when the trees are in bloom, makes her think of a snow-covered hillside. On the way home she might take them down to see the springs and the new springhouse.

Janet and her houseguests are not the only ones: teachers bring schoolchildren there on class trips, mothers come with babies and picnics, and at night there are lovers with blankets and bottles of wine. Herb Davison says that a lot of the visitors like to poke around among the ferns where they guess that the bottling plant used to be, looking for pieces of the old bottles or, better yet, a bottle unbroken, maybe even one with the paper label that tells of the cure and believes in the magic of the springs.
– October 1984

Boston's North

OLD MEN WITH FINE-boned, well-preserved faces sit in folding chairs in doorways and on the street, smoking slowly or eating an orange. There are black-garbed grandmothers making their rounds with expandable string bags, and children and cats darting through alleyways. The men play boccie when the weather gets warm. On summer evenings people come from miles around to take an espresso and pastry or Italian ice, or to enjoy a multicourse Italian meal.

In Boston's kaleidoscopic North End, a people-packed tip of land easing into Boston Harbor, there are over 14,000 people, mostly Italian-Americans, along with everything Italians consider important, especially food.

Irresistible aromas waft from bakeries, restaurants, espresso bars, groceries, butcher shops, and small stores specializing in lavish assortments of dried fruit, salted nuts, and chocolate. There are visions of dark roast coffee beans, crusty loaves, peppery garlic sausage, hunks of aged Romano and Parmesan cheese, hot Sicilian pizza, and cannoli being piped full of fresh ricotta filling.

The North End is known as a safe place to walk, even alone, even for

Women watch the streets from their apartment windows (above) *while youth* (right) *display their form: Dom Francesca, Arthur Wanasa, and twins Robert and Richard Bruno.*

End

by Lynda Morgenroth • Photographs by John Robaton

As an earlier Salem Street vendor (top) did in 1933, Steve Scalafani (above) peddles wares to passers-by. At the end of August, the Feast of St. Anthony (right) turns streets into carnivals.

women, even after dark. It's safe because everyone knows everyone else in the North End. As one shopkeeper puts it, "We keep an eye on people and know who's from outside." The preeminent sentries are the women watching from apartment windows — an excellent strategic position. They zealously guard their children, alerting them to trouble before they know it's there. ("I see a puddle, Mario. *I see it from here.* Watch your step!")

The Italians came to Boston some 90 years ago and have turned the North End into a veritable Mediterranean community. But side by side with pizzeria and espresso bar are vestiges of the immigrants who preceded them — the Puritans, blacks, Irish, and Jews.

Reminders of early Yankees are

The Feast of St. Anthony is only one of ten different festivals celebrated each summer in the North End. Many of these feast days are cause for local residents to display elaborate offerings to religious figures. Combinations of images and money are commonly seen, as the one being prepared to hang from the window here.

low), which is the oldest existing church building in Boston (1723), and Saint Stephen's, designed by Charles Bulfinch in 1804 and originally called the North Meeting House (it became a Roman Catholic church in 1862).

It's harder to find traces of the blacks, Irish, and Jews, but they were North Enders, too. Many of the graves on Copp's Hill Burying Ground — the second oldest cemetery in Boston — belong to slaves and freedmen who were relegated to the Snowhill Street side. Rose Fitzgerald Kennedy was born in 1890 in a brick tenement at 4 Garden Court, and during the second half of the 19th century Salem Street was a veritable Hester Street, filled with Jewish merchants and street peddlers, the hub of Boston's Jewish community.

During the 1920s, younger Jews made their way to the suburbs, as did younger Italians during the 1950s and '60s. "They wanted a grass lawn and a backyard for kids," shrugs Fred Langone, the outspoken 61-year-old Boston City Councilman who's lived in the North End most of his life.

Councilman Langone affectionately describes his neighborhood as "one of the most congested places in the world, probably second only to the Casbah and certain parts of Calcutta." But the character of the old neighborhood is changing. Its ambience has drawn affluent young professionals, many of whom live in the adjacent waterfront area, which some consider part of the North End and some do not. Rents have skyrocketed. The North End isn't as Italian anymore. "The way the North End is — its specialness — is starting to go out," says Dolly Savino Romano, program director at the North End Union, a community service and recreation center. "It's the old people that keep it Italian, the ones with vowels at the end of their names.

"But I'm a city person and could never live anywhere else," she adds. "I'm still fascinated by my own culture. We're close to each other in the North End. If it's 'congested' as some say, that only makes for more conversation and communication. People like it here because they want to believe that neighborhoods still exist. The new people love it for the same reasons we do. It's *fun.* You never know when a parade will go by." *– May 1983*

there too: Paul Revere's house, the only 17th-century dwelling still standing in a big American city; the Moses Pierce-Hitchborn House, an 18th-century building that belonged to Revere's cousin; and Clough House, once inhabited by Ebenezer Clough, a member of the Sons of Liberty who war-painted his face and participated in the Boston Tea Party. There are remarkable churches, including Christ Church ("Old North," made famous by Paul Revere and Henry Wadsworth Longfel-

Angelo and Arpitio Pagliuca take in the scene in front of the Torrese Club, an Italian-American social club.

Rangeley, Maine

YOU SEE THE RED-HAIRED kid catching a red-finned skinner from the brook that flows through town. You note the elderly woman, surrounded by geraniums and midday stillness, doing a crossword puzzle on her front porch, which is just up Main Street from Doc Grant's Restaurant and the nice fresh turkey sandwiches they serve there.

You visit a few of the "camps" on the shore of Rangeley Lake and observe the fine antiques and leatherbound books and the other details of quiet wealth. Then you spend the night in a lakeside log building that was built 60 years ago with the same care and craftsmanship one finds in a fine old clock. Rangeley has the presence of no other Maine town. You sense this the first time you visit, and the feeling gets stronger each time you come back. It is unlike Greenville and Jackman, rugged inland settlements, because Rangeley is as elegant as it is rugged. It is unlike Prouts Neck and Christmas Cove, wealthy enclaves on the coast, because Rangeley, while most civilized, is rough-cut.

If you are truly curious about this lakeside town in Franklin County and you start asking around, Gus Hinkley is a good place to start. Born on a small Rangeley dairy farm, he is something of a local historian. He disappears into his barn and returns with an armful of files. From them and him, you begin to understand.

Only 170 years ago, what is now Rangeley was a wilderness untouched, uncut, and unfished by white settlers. Then about 1815 a man with the sober-sounding name of Deacon Luther appeared dragging his hand sled, two bushels of grain, and his family (including an infant who traveled in a bread bin).

Deacon Luther began what was to be his and the following settlers' dominant activity in the Rangeley Lake district for the next half century — homestead-

by Jack Aley • Photographs by Stephen O. Muskie

Before the morning fog has burned off Rangeley Lake, two fishermen try their luck by a small dam just off Route 4.

ing and clearing the land by hand.

By 1862, according to Hinkley's account, there was still no actual town of Rangeley, but rather a loosely defined community held together by the business of survival. By that year, however, the area's first inn had been built about three miles east of where Rangeley lies today. It was called the Greenvale House.

Three men came to stay at the Greenvale House in the year 1862, a visit that was to change forever the course of events in the wilderness settlements. They were not settlers in search of subsistence. They were three men from Massachusetts: Ira Leonard, Samuel Rivers, and a man called Jacob. They had come by stagecoach to fish for sport, and they found a sportsman's paradise.

Back to their more settled state, Rangeley's first recorded sportsmen took tales of the countless lake and brook trout and salmon to be caught in lakes of incomparable beauty. The word about Rangeley spread quickly among a select class of fishermen. And so fly fishermen started making pilgrimages to Rangeley.

Fly fishing, as much art as it is sport, represents a union of an exacting process, discerning creatures, and painstaking individuals. Rangeley, as a mecca for fly fishing, began to take on the sport's artfulness.

By 1900, fly fishermen, the reigning purists of sport, had created in Rangeley a place of unmistakable tone, or, as one local put it, "a grandiose experience." Every summer, from places like Philadelphia, Boston, and New York, the judges and doctors and politicians and musicians and writers and their families would arrive by train, with great trunks filled with enough goods to live in the grand manner for an entire season. They moved into the great hotels, which had been built on Rangeley Lake, or into the elegantly rustic camps on the shores of Rangeley, Mooselookmeguntic, Kennebago, or one of the other superb lakes in the region.

These sport fishermen, who seldom ate the trout they caught, were not con-

Out before the early fishermen, these three ducks have City Cove, near Rangeley's center, all to themselves.

tent with the wild place settled by Deacon Luther. Instinctively they used their wealth and deployed their tastes, and slowly but surely Rangeley began to take on its ethereal difference. The fly fishermen wanted from Rangeley not only a place to fish but also a retreat — and nothing too crude, thank you. In myriad and subtle ways, Rangeley began to reflect the essence of a ritual sport and the sophistication of the people drawn to that sport.

The rarefied nature of fly fishing itself, plus the remoteness of Rangeley, helped maintain the area's exclusiveness for decades. Invitations to join the "club" were sent out discreetly on the "old boy" network. It was not until the 1940s that the "tin-can crowd," as one old-style camp owner dubbed them, started arriving on the newly improved roads.

RANGELEY, MAINE

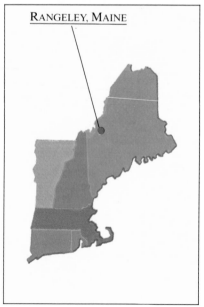

For early sports (above), *the lure of Rangeley was its great fishing. For Californians Dick and JoAnn Menard* (right), *watching a sunset on Lake Mooselookmeguntic is enough.*

The new roads, to be sure, set the stage for some changes in Rangeley. The grand old hotels, for example, are gone and have been replaced by not-so-grand motels. But much of the feel and the substance of pre-tin-can Rangeley endures. The traditions implanted by the fishermen with the dry flies were strong ones. Indirectly but unmistakably, fly fishing zoned Rangeley. "Fly fishing," observed a contemporary practitioner of the art, "is going to stop a certain class of people from coming to Rangeley. Fly fishing is not democratic; it is aristocratic."

– September 1984

Aroostook County, Maine

by Mel Allen • Photographs by Carole Allen

THINGS ARE CHANGING rapidly here in Aroostook County, Maine — too rapidly, folks say — but what hasn't changed is you still need a whole lot of luck to make a go of it growing potatoes.

This is big country, larger than Connecticut and Rhode Island combined, nearly the equal of Massachusetts; its vastness is more suggestive of the West than of New England. Its winters, people tell you, are fiercer, its forests thicker, its rivers wilder than anywhere else in the East. Many of its towns are as far removed from Portland (Maine's largest city) as Portland is from New York City, and the differences are no less striking.

During potato harvest big numbers roll off the tongue easily: 2.5 billion pounds of potatoes raised on 124,000 acres; 1,000 growers needing 22,000 workers; thousands of dollars may be gained or lost in a single day's price fluctuation. It is easy to lose yourself in these numbers, to forget that all numbers reduce to a grower and his workers against the cold blustery days sure to follow.

I have come to help with the harvest — at best it should be a way to enjoy the Aroostook autumn while earning up to $20 a day and keeping fit. At worst it should be a relatively painless way to join a unique indigenous culture, unmatched elsewhere in New England. My grower is Donald Gallagher. He farms the land his father farmed, living still where his father lived. He picks his words carefully, taking pleasure in his pipe. Like others who live by the land, it is impossible to imagine him dressed in anything other than overalls and workshirt, a blue cap tugged low on his forehead.

Don Gallagher grows potatoes for seed. While Idaho, Washington, and North Dakota continue to crowd Maine potatoes from the table stock and processing markets, no other state grows more seed potatoes than Maine. People in Michigan or Arkansas depend on Gallagher to grow potatoes that are perfect.

While friends are switching from harvesting potatoes by hand to two-row mechanical harvesters that replace at least 22 pickers, Gallagher knows potatoes picked by machine are four times as likely to bruise. So each morning he starts his old yellow school bus and heads down Route 169 between Presque Isle and Fort Fairfield picking up school kids (who are let out of school for the harvest) as he has for years.

There's no easy way to pick potatoes. There never was and there never will be. You bend over, put the basket between your legs and move forward, picking with both hands. As long as you keep moving you won't stiffen up. Your legs go first, then your back. But more painful than either is when your wrists begin to swell. For a few days you feel terrible. Then you get used to it and concentrate on filling barrels at 40 cents a barrel.

Be patient and look around. It is early and the sun has not yet risen above the distant maples. The pickers wear sweaters, but within an hour sweaters lie strewn like fallen leaves.

It is a time of intense activity, yet a time also of waiting. Youngsters help neighbors clean up their sections while waiting for the digger to clank their way again. Potato trucks roar into the fields spewing dust. Every 15-year-old waits to turn 16 — to work the machines, to drive the trucks. Barrels laden with potatoes are hoisted onto the trucks with grapples, empty ones flung to the earth.

Time goes so slowly. I watch a girl walk towards a hillock and think it is noon; it is only 9:30. Half-starved, you wait for lunch. If it's your style you tear off chunks of raw potatoes. There are some who say they are best that way.

Lunch time. The pickers make idle gossip sitting between rows like barrels. Occasionally a potato whips by, followed by farm-country insults: "Dumber than a tumbleweed," or "Number than a hammered thumb." I marvel at the energy of those who use this time for play.

You listen for the digger beginning its clanking call back to work. Though it means money lost, you half await sounds of malfunction, sounds that mean repairs. You watch the sun slipping away, while feeling for muscles in your back that once, a long time ago, seemed a part of you. You wait for the last truck to deliver the last empty barrels; hitch a ride on the back of the truck to the bus in the next field.

People here say I am witnessing the end of an era, that within five years the hand-harvesting of potatoes will be ancient history. Though the work is hard and tedious, I begin to understand the sadness with which they say this.

Older people speak of picking potatoes as though these fields were the playgrounds of their youth. On Satur-

Teenagers earn cash by bending to the task of picking potatoes on Don Gallagher's farm in Presque Isle.

Like all Aroostook potato farmers, Don Gallagher (right) *spends much of the harvest season worrying. While he hired pickers to harvest the crop, his neighbor Robert McBurnie has switched to a mechanical harvester* (far right). *A break in the work* (below) *means a chance for greeting a companion.*

days you see them still, kerchiefs wrapped around their heads, kneeling beside their children, moving crablike along the ground.

"Our kids have learned there's no easy money," said a mother of two. "They're not afraid of hard work. Picking potatoes has put iron in their soup and we're proud of them. It will be a sorry time to see it disappear."

If, indeed, the hand-harvesting of potatoes disappears, it will be a victim of cultural as well as economic pressures. It costs a grower a dollar more per barrel to harvest by hand. But as Herschel Smith, the county's largest private grower, said, "I'd still pick all mine by hand if I could. Hand-picked potatoes

are better, just as hand-knitted sweaters are better."

Physically, the changes are already evident. You are as likely to see school kids working in fast-food restaurants during harvest as in the fields. Flatbed trucks that for years roared down the narrow roads with full loads of 60 barrels are being replaced by ponderous bulk bodies; linked to mechanical harvesters, they hold 40 barrels more. Potato houses dug deep into the earth that have given this area its distinctive appearance are now out of date, too awkward for unloading bulk bodies.

What has not changed, though, is the worry. During these final September days it blows across the land like potato

dust. This big country has big worries to match. To worry is a way of life, but you never get used to it. Said the wife of Robert McBurnie, who farms near Don Gallagher, "When we get them out we're really different people."

Worry about ring rot, about water rot, about black leg, about the blight. Worry about Idaho growing too many potatoes, about Europe not needing enough. Worry about a frost coming too soon for early Superiors, or too late to kill the tops of later Russets. Worry about pickers leaving, about machines breaking. Most of them, though, can handle the worry. What they can't handle this harvest is the rain.

There is a different quality to the rain

here. Someone said it is the sweat of the farmers that makes it so. The soil is porous limestone shale. In a normal year it can absorb an inch of rain during the night and be dry by noon.

But in this abnormal year it rains night and day. During the second harvest week many growers are lucky to harvest six hours. The mood of these restive men and women becomes as somber as the sky.

For diversion people go to the Aroostook River and watch it turn brown from their soil. Nine tons of topsoil per acre is washed away each year. The farmers know about soil conservation, about crop rotation, about burning up the soil too rapidly. But they are

trapped by debts and competition, and the river grows chocolate with their life's blood. The Commission on Maine's Future predicts that within 25 years there may be no more potato farming in Aroostook County.

"I can't worry about 25 years from now," a farmer sighed. "I'm still worrying about yesterday."

"It's survival of the fittest," one grower said. "Whether you till today or tomorrow may mean the difference between profit and loss. All it takes is a couple of poorly planned years to put you under. The bad farmers get weeded out fast. We're getting down to fewer and better growers who have been through the wringer."

It has rained again during the night. When Donald Gallagher checked his rain gauge in the morning, more than an inch had fallen. That night the winds had come with the rain, too, and ripped through the bare land.

Before the storm the sky was clear, and shooting stars flared. The air was moist and sweet and I knew again what the constant rain had made me forget, why Aroostook people say they would live nowhere else, why they hold onto their land with the tenacity of wolves.

Don Gallagher works on his digger, hoping the ground will dry by noon. He finds it almost impossible now to find new parts for his digger and he ponders its repair. Though his fields are miser-

To accommodate the harvest, school recesses for three weeks in September.

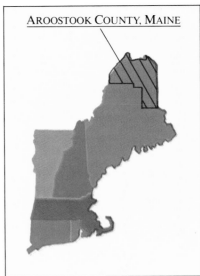

AROOSTOOK COUNTY, MAINE

able with mud he's willing to give it a try later.

There are woods behind his house and he walks there trying to decide. He points out the spring where he has drunk since boyhood, and moose and deer tracks around a wild, golden apple tree. He bites into an apple. He wants to show me where, as a boy, he scratched his initials on an outcropping of rocks, but the rocks are covered with moss.

A year before, Gallagher and all his neighbors had a boom year. An average grower received $12 a barrel, some as much as $20. Some growers with only 100 acres paid over $8,000 in income taxes. Growers figure it costs them nearly $7 a barrel to plant, harvest, store, and ship potatoes. Already the talk is gloomy. "We'll be lucky to get $5 a barrel," the talk goes. Gallagher suspects it will be lower than that, and a few months later he is proven correct.

He walks across the road to his fields. He's dismayed at the barrels left in disarray, but mostly he is dismayed at the sodden ground. Potatoes are drowning at his feet. In six months, farmers will be calling this "the worst year since the Depression."

The elms and maples are already half bare of leaves on the perimeter of his land. He says we might have a chance to see foliage in the St. John Valley if only the rain would stop. We have been speaking of the inevitable changes in Aroostook. He takes out his ever-present pocketknife and silently cleans his pipe. Then he says quietly, "They don't know what they're losin'."

– *September 1978*

Rhode Island

by James Dodson • Photographs by Ulrike Welsch

In Watch Hill, the word "cottage" has especially elegant connotations.

ONCE UPON A TIME A traveling circus came to Watch Hill, Rhode Island, a small town by the sea. It was so long ago no one remembers when the circus came or how long it stayed, but the convenient estimate is that it showed up one day in late summer about a hundred years ago. Some claim the circus was run by gypsies who ran out of money by the time they reached Watch Hill and simply vanished, leaving no trace of themselves except a lovely wooden flying-horse carousel.

Sea winds and social change have altered Watch Hill since then, but the flying-horse carousel still stands and still operates — a gentle affront to time and evolution at the corner of Larken and Bay streets, not a hundred feet from the edge of the Atlantic Ocean. The horses of the carousel are small, but each is carved from a solid piece of wood and has a real leather saddle and its original agate eyes.

It seems fitting that the precise origins of the carousel remain a mystery, for a certain romance has always pervaded the village of Watch Hill, a select summer spa chosen by good families and old money for its relative remoteness from the hustle and grind of the outside world. A carousel left by a vanished circus acts as the perfect centerpiece. For two bits a child can still be borne around by a wooden horse.

In Watch Hill life is weather and memory. The feeling of durable families, the glimpse of croquet mallets left on a wide lawn, a child's blond head visible in the garden — these are what visitors expect. But in Watch Hill there is also Snuffy Conto, unelected mayor *de facto,* ambassador of local color, purveyor of the Italian sausage omelet. Short, olive-skinned, he is a father of four and grandfather of five, all of whom have worked the unpretentious floor or kitchen of Snuffy's restaurant on Bay Street, the main drag in Watch Hill. There is no town hall and no police station (the village is a part of the town of Westerly) — only a blinking caution light, a single fire station, a collection of shops and restaurants, and Snuffy and his goofy bow ties.

"How many of those things do you own?" he is asked by a visitor.

Snuffy contemplates a moment, then shoots a gummy smile. "Three hundred and fifty," he answers, touching the one he has on. "Maybe close to four hundred now. God bless you."

In 1955, when Snuffy Conto opened his place in Watch Hill, the trolley tracks still ran along Bay Street, ending at the carousel. Exactly one hundred years before that, a man named George Nash erected a mammoth wooden hotel called The Atlantic House on the rocky promontory above the mouth of the Pawcatuck River, which divides Rhode Island from Connecticut.

In 1884 a syndicate of Cincinnati businessmen began buying up land around Watch Hill and fashioning impressive summer "cottages" for wealthy visitors eager to have a New England roosting place. Many came from the Midwest and South, and one migrating bird brought another. By the turn of the century there were seven grand hotels — including The Plimpton, The Narragansett, The Watch Hill, and The Ocean House — on the elevated shores, along with many sumptuous private homes. It was, as one longtime resident put it, "a golden age of gardeners and little girls playing on the lawn."

**Popular myth has it that gypsies
left this wooden flying-horse
carousel when they ran out of money.**

**By the turn of the century, seven grand
hotels perched on Little Narragansett Bay.**

Snuffy Conto, the unelected mayor, with one of his famous bow ties.

Little Narragansett Bay, the village's protected harbor, became a desired mooring place for the privileged: Andrew Mellon and Henry Ford kept large yachts there. Douglas Fairbanks, Groucho Marx, Isadora Duncan, Clark Gable, and David Niven were among those drawn to the hushed lawns and privacy of Watch Hill. But others came, too — daytrippers who could at least nose around and ride the carousel. At one time, a steamboat made 17 round trips a day from Westerly.

One morning in September 1938, a young local man named Andy Pupillo was helping out a prominent family named Moore with odd jobs — earning a few bucks before going back to the University of Connecticut, where he was a senior and a star athlete. The wind suddenly came up, bringing a wall of rain at high tide. Pupillo and the Moores went inside to wait out the storm. All around them the houses of Watch Hill were washing away. Pupillo rescued the family's 12-year-old son from the garage, then shepherded everyone up to the third floor of the house. The windows blew out, and when the second floor suddenly collapsed they were in the water, 11 people huddled in the remains of a house, swept out to sea. Some time later, miraculously, the "raft" washed up on the Connecticut side of the Pawcatuck. Pu-

Watch Hill's one public beach is beginning to strain under the growing population of daytripping tourists.

pillo, his shoulder broken, managed to get the stunned members of the Moore family arranged under a bale of straw to wait out the night. He cradled their chilled five-year-old daughter in his own arms. Later, he was the only one who refused to go to the hospital.

In all, 59 houses and the beach club of Watch Hill were blown away by the hurricane of '38, and 15 area people were killed. The flying-horse carousel survived almost unscathed, buried like Pompeii, though under tons of sand instead of ash. But Andy Pupillo never returned to college. Sand in his lungs brought on tuberculosis, and he died less than two years later in a Boston hospital.

Jessie Pupillo Holdredge, who with her husband Charlie operated the only gas station in Watch Hill for many years, was reminded of her brother's heroism recently when an account of the tragedy turned up, written by Andy less than two weeks before he died. For her, it opened up other channels of memory. She remembered the man who ambled into her garage in 1946 to ask directions. They talked, and she conducted the stranger around the village. The man, Albert Einstein, came back to Watch Hill three summers in a row, and always stopped in to see Jessie and Charlie.

In 1954, she recalled, Hurricane Carol filled Watch Hill's main street with water, but Jessie and Charlie stayed because a local captain told them "it wouldn't be too bad a blow." Thinking of that now, Jessie smiles. "Thank God he was right, because we stayed."

There are, Jessie explains, no more Fords or Mellons in Watch Hill, but the great houses are still there. They belong to the scions of chemical companies, railroads, and tobacco fortunes now. For the most part, these people remain out of sight behind their hedges. "They wouldn't mind if you photographed their houses," Jessie observes, "but they would never let you take their pictures." Privacy is what Watch Hill is all about to some people.

And that is where conflict has developed. On any given summer day as many as 10,000 tourists come to Watch Hill. To some residents, the T-shirt shops and ice cream vendors that moved in to capitalize on the daily rush of sun worshipers are a real annoyance. To others, that sort of commerce is a necessary fact of life. The argument is neither new nor uncommon in coastal New England towns these days. Watch Hill has limited resources — one small public beach, a couple of private beaches where visitors are allowed, a few free on-street parking places, and three small parking lots.

"The real question is one of moderation and fairness," argues Jack Fulber, who bought the Olympia Tea Room on Bay Street a few years ago. "Watch Hill has always been a family place, and even with all of the changes in it, the intention of most people will be to keep it that way. In summer there are about 300 families living here. Many of them have nothing to do with the businesses on Bay Street. But there are other people who make their livings off the tourists. Is that so bad? In winter there are less than 100 families living out here. Our light, and the light at Jessie's garage, are the only lights shining on the street. We have a substantial stake in Watch Hill, too."

For her part, Jessie Holdredge is feeling a bit the way she did when the captain told her Hurricane Carol was coming ashore in 1954. Her husband Charlie died not long ago, and within two weeks of his burial she had been visited at least seven times by real estate people who thought she might be interested in selling. One woman came back several times. "She was so persistent — even insistent — and told me she could get me big bucks if I'd agree to sell. Big

Jessie Holdredge (left) sits in her rocker down at the garage she runs and recalls her brother Andy's (above) heroism during the hurricane of 1938. He saved 11 members of the Moore family but then died two years later as a result of sand that he had inhaled during the rescue of the family.

The hurricane of 1938 destroyed 59 cottages, like this one washed clear across Watch Hill Pond.

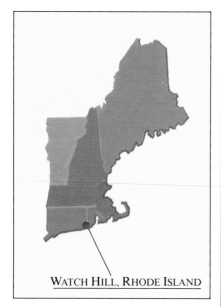

bucks. Watch Hill is very hot. That's exactly how she said it," Holdredge reports with mild contempt. "I told her I have all the money I need, thank you, and she looked at me as if I were an idiot or something."

"Listen," Snuffy Conto insists. "Everybody wants to come back to Watch Hill once they been here. You can't blame them. I been here —" he pauses to think, touching a blunt finger to his bow tie again — "I been here 40-something years, and I've seen 'em come and go. Ask Snuffy. He knows. I think they *should* come, too. They come, they stay, and then they go. God bless them." He shrugs.

Outside, the daytrippers are packing up the Coleman stoves, and the sun is melting redly over the mouth of the Mystic River a few miles to the west. If one watches long enough, young girls with wheaty, sun-ripened hair begin to emerge again on the secret lawns of Watch Hill. This is a magical time — a space between night and day. For the moment, the present is held in thrall to the past. Life here, one senses, is still weather and memories. Down at her little garage, Jessie Holdredge is in her mission rocker, savoring the sea breeze. She won't be going anywhere soon. At the other end of Bay Street, the flying-horse carousel goes around for the final time today. Its sweet-sad music lingers in the air, a song with no name, and can be heard as far down as Jessie's place when the wind is just right.

– June 1986

The view from the Ocean House porch preserves a 19th-century grandeur.

The Cornwalls of Connecticut

by Laurie O'Neill • Photographs by Donald Pahl Heiny

WHEN IT'S SO QUIET that you can hear the Housatonic River rushing under the red covered bridge, you know it's not quite summer in West Cornwall. A pair of guinea hens scratch for food in the dirt parking lot of Yutzler's Country Store. Mary Woodman rests her elbows on the counter of the tiny post office, its windows filled with leggy geraniums, to chat with a customer. Two boys pick their way along a trestle of the abandoned Housatonic Railroad.

By July the village will have come to life. Yutzler's lot will be jammed, and owners Phil and Jane Bishop will be kept busy weighing produce, slicing cheese, and wrapping meat. The hens, indignant, will flee, squawking, to a distant abutment.

"It used to be you knew everybody in town," laments Thalia Scoville, whose husband Ralph, a former selectman, runs the 225-acre dairy farm that has been in his family for five generations. "Now," she says, "there are so many strange faces."

But summer people are hardly a new phenomenon in this northwestern Connecticut community, 48.8 square miles of hills and valleys crossed by winding country roads, and so picturesque that it has been described as "a half mile from heaven." Since the mid-1800s, when householders began taking in summer boarders, city people have been drawn to Cornwall as a rustic retreat. By the turn of the century, the visitors began buying up old farms and residences or building summer homes. There are some 300 part-time residents now.

The relative seclusion Cornwall offers its residents is due to the fact that the town is still heavily wooded and has no single center — no "downtown" or Main Street. Cornwall is three villages, four miles apart, each with its own post office. Cornwall Plains, also called "the Village," is a pristine arrangement of late 18th- and early 19th-century homes built around a common green. In the Plains are the town offices, public library, historical society, two churches, a private secondary school, and a dairy farm, all overlooking Coltsfoot Valley and the Cathedral Pines, a majestic, 42-acre stand of 150- to 300-year-old white pines that a village family, the Calhouns, deeded to The Nature Conservancy 17 years ago.

West Cornwall — with its art studios and café in the old railroad depot, its antiques shop and crafts boutique, its corner restaurant that serves quiche and homemade muffins, and its resident cabinetmaker in the old toll house on the riverbank — is considered to be Cornwall's most eclectic settlement. Cornwall Bridge, on busy Route 7, is the town's commercial center, providing the other Cornwalls with everyday necessities.

There are four other Cornwalls: Cornwall Centre (the town's first settlement and former site of a school, church, stocks and pillory, tavern, and parade ground), East Cornwall, North Cornwall, and Cornwall Hollow. Other areas include Yelping Hill, established as a summer colony of artists, writers, and educators in the 1920s; Cream Hill, where one of the country's first agricultural schools thrived in the mid-1800s; and Dark Entry, whose residents have formed an association to protect the land.

Like other country towns that have

Yelping Hill was established in Cornwall as a summer artists' colony in the 1920s. The influence persists, because even today the town is a favorite subject for painters.

Taking part in a road race sponsored by a local group, racers hustle their bicycles through Cornwall Bridge.

– courtesy The Cornwall (Ct.) Historical Society

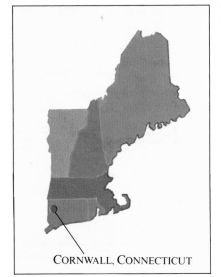

CORNWALL, CONNECTICUT

This 1859 engraving (above) of the Gold residence in Cream Hill shows the site of one of this country's first agricultural schools. The Dormitory is behind the main house and sports a cupola and flagpole. A young bystander (left) supports a whimsical sign warning motorists of a huge puddle in front of West Cornwall train station.

been "discovered" by outsiders, Cornwall is attempting to prevent unbridled development. "We're holding on longer, that's what makes Cornwall different from other towns," contends Harriet Clark, a former teacher, state legislator, and local historian.

Robert T. Beers, who visited Cornwall as a child, began weekending there after World War II, and retired with his wife Mary to Cream Hill in 1976, only to wind up being elected first selectman. Beers says, "The town hasn't changed all that much. I'd have to say it's an ideal community."

– July 1984

Local historian Harriet Clark, seated, with her sister and nephew on her family homestead, Mohawk Farm.

DAVID BALDWIN HOUSE 1743
—
J.I. NEWTON TAVERN 1840
—
CLARK HOMESTEAD 1865

The Towns of Mount

OFF TO THE SIDE OF NEW Hampshire's corridor of cities — Nashua, Manchester, Concord — bordered on the west by Vermont and on the south by Massachusetts, the 46 towns in the lower corner of New Hampshire make up what some call "the quiet corner." A web of towns 50 miles square, the Monadnock Region includes Alstead, Antrim, Ashuelot, Bennington, Chesham, Chesterfield, Deering, Dublin, Fitzwilliam, Francestown, Gilsum, Greenfield, Greenville, Hancock, Harrisville, Hillsboro, Hinsdale, Jaffrey, Jaffrey Center, Keene, Lyndeborough, Marlborough, Marlow, Mason, Milford, Munsonville, Nelson, New Ipswich, Peterborough, Richmond, Rindge, Roxbury, Sharon, Spofford, Stoddard, Sullivan, Surry, Swanzey, Temple, Troy, Walpole, West Chesterfield, Westmoreland, West Swanzey, Wilton, and Winchester.

It is wooded, hilly countryside, where many of the towns, like Nelson and Francestown and Westmoreland, come as a surprise around a sharp curve. Many of the town centers are simply a post office and a general store surrounded by white, clapboarded houses. All but nine of these towns have fewer than 1,000 residents, a smallness that is, for the most part, treasured. Here towns stand stern on the question of widening roads and letting interstates pass through. There are no interstates to link the towns of the Monadnock Region. What does tie all these towns together is the mountain.

A single peak rising above soft hills, Mount Monadnock is neighbor to all these towns. It can be seen from each of them. From the farthest, such as Alstead 25 miles north or Winchester 25 miles southwest, the mountain is a glimpse, a distant peak that can be seen only from an upstairs bedroom window in houses faced just right on the higher hills. But from Jaffrey or Dub-

After school, children play amid the foliage in New Ipswich, a town famed for its many beautiful old homes.

Monadnock

by Edie Clark
Photographs by Carole Allen

Good weather in foliage season brings hundreds of hikers to the open summit of Mt. Monadnock, at 3,165 feet the dominant peak for miles around.

lin, the mountain is a presence. Magnificent views come often, around many corners, across open fields. The best view is a subject of debate and fine-tuned comparison: "It's best on the road to Troy." "No, it's better from the Old Harrisville Road. From there you can see the hills on either side."

The mountain is a stretch of granite five miles long and four miles across. Up until the early 1800s, when forest fires and subsequent erosion stripped it clean, it was forested right to the summit. The word "monadnock" (a geological term meaning "a hill or mountain of resistant rock surrounded by a peneplain") is listed in the dictionary, and this mountain is credited as the word's derivation.

Although the first trail was cut in 1706, hikers with no more than a pleasant day in mind began trekking to the summit in the early 1800s, carrying wicker picnic baskets and peering at the view through spyglasses. Word spread of the mountain's accessibility and its view: some could pick out their towns or their lakes and, when the weather was good, they could pick out Boston to the southeast as well as

October light strikes a Fitzwilliam dooryard *(above)*. **Postcard circa 1900** *(right)* **shows a couple in idyllic repose on Monadnock's summit.**

Hillside fields dot region, many offering views of the mountain. These horses in Dublin found the photographer more intriguing than Monadnock.

Mount Washington, 105 miles to the north.

Over the years the mountain has inspired many canvases and scores of poems. Emerson, Hawthorne, Whittier, Thoreau, Mark Twain — all had something to say, most of it rapturous, about this mountain. Willa Cather, who came from Nebraska and wrote so evocatively of the flat plains of the Midwest, is buried by choice near the base of Mount Monadnock, in Jaffrey Center.

Monadnock, it might seem, has earned an esteem out of proportion to its height. At 3,165 feet, Monadnock doesn't even come close to making it onto the list of the nation's highest peaks: on a list of the 70 highest mountains in the United States, the last one listed comes in at 14,048 feet. But Monadnock rivals Japan's Fuji (12,389 feet) as the world's most-climbed mountain. A single fall day can attract as many as a thousand hikers. The park service expects between 125,000 and 150,000 hikers each year — a rough estimate, since many hikers take trails not monitored by the park.

Ten such trails are cared for by the park service. By the most direct trail,

– Courtesy Dan Johnson Collection

climbers can reach the summit in less than three hours. The trails are not difficult: children are regular climbers on all routes. The paths, narrow and wooded near the base, wind across blueberry ledges, then rise steeply along granite stepping stones, and soon emerge above the timberline where the breeze comes up most days, refreshing as a drink of water.

Many people who live in the towns that surround the mountain have climbed it hundreds of times. Some hike the mountain once a week or more to stay fit and because they love the view, which sets up the Monadnock Region like a map in relief.

William House lives near the mountain in Harrisville. His windows boast a straightforward view of Monadnock's north side. The walls of his den are hung with pictures of high, high mountain peaks, their rocky faces streaked with midsummer snow. Mr. House is a mountaineer who reached 26,000 feet in a 1938 expedition onto K2, a peak

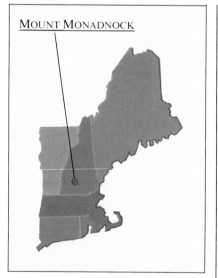

MOUNT MONADNOCK

adjacent to Mount Everest. He was part of the first ascent of Mount Waddington in British Columbia and the first to climb Devil's Tower in Wyoming. Today, at 69, he enjoys hiking Mount Monadnock.

Small-scale sheep farming is returning (above) *to what was once a great sheep raising area. Older, gentler ways of harvesting timber* (right) *are finding favor in hillside woodlots, as well.*

He prefers to climb in the late fall, when the bugs are gone and the leaves have fallen, sharpening the view. "It's a good mountain, because you can get up above the timberline very quickly," he says. Looking down from the bony summit, the hills seem close, and the shapes of the many lakes and ponds are distinguishable. He picks out Silver Lake, shaped like a hand with a finger pointing north, and moves his field glasses southeast until he comes to the field in front of his house. The weathered wood siding of the house blends with its wooded backdrop, but on a clear day he can almost always make out its shape. In this way, Mount Monadnock gives him what no other mountain can: from the top he can see his home.
– October 1982

Wilsons Mills, Maine

NOBODY KNOWS WHERE the idea came from to feed wild deer, but the practice goes back before the memory of longtime residents. "I can remember my grandfather and my aunt feeding hay to the deer. That was, oh, more than 40 years ago," says Norman Littlehale. Wilsons Mills, one of the smallest and most remote towns in the country, might just be the only place in the nation where a motorist can count on seeing wild deer in significant numbers without ever leaving his car. The town spent $2,500 for deer feed in 1983, a considerable sum for a community with fewer than 50 people.

It used to be you couldn't get there from Maine without going to New Hampshire first. Wilsons Mills is on the Magalloway River, some 1,500 feet above sea level right near the border of the tippity top of New Hampshire. It's 45 miles to the nearest movie theater, the nearest supermarket. TV reception is limited to Channel 8 on Mount Washington. The closest community of any size is Berlin, New Hampshire, an hour's drive away on winding roads. It wasn't until the 1930s, when Route 16 was extended, that Wilsons Mills was connected to the rest of Maine by auto road.

The land here is granite strewn, the river valley narrow. Forests have overgrown the farmlands. The trees are mainly spruce and fir, giving the hills a permanent Christmasy look. There's water everywhere — ponds, lakes, bogs, rivers, streams. It's cold, too, and the blackflies stay until the middle of August. The deer — which the town feeds only during the hard winter months — are here all year long.

One of the deer feeding stations is across the road from the Don and Donna Glover house, the former Aziscoos Hotel. Donna's favorite deer was Shot Foot, named because of a wound in his leg. The leg healed over until it looked like a gnarled root. The Glovers watched

Don Glover carries out the public duty, feeding the deer at one of Wilsons Mills' four feeding stations.

by Ernie Hebert • Photographs by Kip Brundage

Students from three towns help each other (above) *in the wood-frame schoolhouse* (right) *in Wilsons Mills.*

Shot Foot for three seasons while he seemed to get weaker, lamer. They found him one day in the woods where he had lain down for the last time. "He died of natural causes. I think he just gave up," says Donna Glover.

William Adams is 78, the oldest native in Wilsons Mills. He tells his deer story:

"I came home one night, thought I wanted to go hunting. So I took my gun, went up through here to the hill. I saw this buck. I shot and, I don't know, I must have broken his back. He cried and he cried and he cried. I said to myself, 'Fella, you don't need it that bad.' I haven't hunted since. I started feeding the deer. I used to take a couple of pails of grain and spread it in piles with a coffee can. The deer, sometimes 30 or 40 at once, would line up for it like cattle. I had one little buck that came four feet

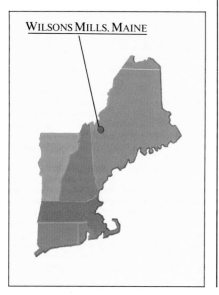

WILSONS MILLS, MAINE

from the window of the house and ate bird seed right out of the feeder. And there was a little doe used to follow my wife everywhere, just like a dog or a cat. After you feed deer, you couldn't hurt one."

A town with a tradition of supplying hunting and fishing guides to down-country sports, Wilsons Mills today has only a handful of deer hunters. Plenty of fly fishermen, though.

The town lies in the shadow of Aziscohos Dam, which holds back 16-mile-long Aziscohos Lake. The "h" in Aziscohos is often absent from place names, and the same goes for the apos-

trophe in Wilsons Mills. The history of the town is interwoven with that of neighboring Magalloway, both towns having been once incorporated into Lincoln Plantation. Magalloway later broke away, but Wilsons Mills is still known in some legal senses as Lincoln Plantation.

Wilsons Mills has a pretty little wood-frame, two-room schoolhouse with eight grades. Teacher and principal Theo Angelini teaches 14 kids, five from Wilsons Mills, seven from Magalloway, and two from the tiny hamlet of Wentworth Location, New Hampshire. Every four years or so the Wilsons Mills school closes down and the kids move to the two-room school in Magalloway, a custom that satisfies the law and local pride. With all eight grades in one room, knowledge spirals down from the top grades to the lower ones, says Mrs. Angelini. Older kids can commute to the high school in Rangeley 30 miles away, or they can attend a high school of their choice even farther away, with the State of Maine paying $40 a week to board each student.

The name of the town comes from John M. Wilson, called Captain Wilson for reasons no one is quite sure of. He was about as tough, persistent — and persistently unlucky — a pioneer as you could find. He launched the town in 1834 when he built a sawmill along the Magalloway. It was swept away by a spring flood. He rebuilt the mill. The second mill burned down. Wilson built again, hence the plural "Mills" in the name of the town. Wilson tried to promote a railroad line from coastal Maine through the Magalloway region to Newport, Vermont. It failed. In his old age, having lost two mills, a number of political battles, and three sons, Wilson moved out. Today there are no Wilson heirs living in the town.

As always, people in Wilsons Mills work in the woods, on the road, in a sporting camp, or way out of town. Eleanor White, for example, is a nurse at the Coos County nursing home in New

Deer in town are certainly well-fed residents, even in a hard winter.

Hampshire, more than 50 miles away. Residents own only about one-eighth of the town, a little more than 3,000 acres. Almost 23,000 acres are held by nonresidents, mainly pulp and lumber companies. There used to be several farms, but they aren't worked today, and the owners live out of town. Local people brood about the farms, wondering what will happen to them. The town has a covered bridge (used to be two), a town hall, an exquisite chapel built with the help of a sportsman patron in 1901, and a fire station. That's it. There's no police department (the town spent $7 on police matters in 1983). Albert Tirrell, the road

surveyor, plows residents' driveways as well as the two miles of town roads.

One resident said Wilsons Mills is a good place to grow up in, to flee from during one's oat-sowing years, and to return to settle down — if you can get a job. People here like their town. They like the quiet, the feeling of freedom, the countryside, the fishing, the clear air, the starry nights, and the almost complete absence of automobile traffic. They say they are grateful to the blackflies for discouraging newcomers to the town.

Alice Harvey, at the Tuesday meeting of the Ladies of the Aziscoos Grange (the Silly Society, as they jokingly call themselves), answers the most frequently asked question of residents of Wilsons Mills: What do you do up here?

"We have a lot of fun," she says, and the other ladies, sitting around the table in the town hall kitchen as they knit, crochet, and make quilts, join in with approving laughter. *– February 1985*

Granville, Vermont

AT AROUND 8:30 ON THE MORN-
ing of March 3, Town Meeting
Day throughout Vermont,
Margaret Handly will lace
up her winter boots, put
a lined nylon windbreaker on over her
heavy sweater, and pull down the flaps
on her wool plaid hunter's cap. She will
go out to the barn to warm up her four-
wheel-drive Ram Charger and wait
there for her neighbor across the street,
Stanford Jarvis, to join her. They will
ride the 45 miles down through Bethel,
west over Route 107, then north into
Rochester and on up to the Granville
town hall. If the weather's not too bad,
they'll get there by 10, just when the
meeting's being called to order. Stanford is one of the town's selectmen and
Margaret is the school director and
town constable. For something like 30
years, Margaret and Stanford have
made this trip together from East
Granville to their town meeting. At
best, they won't return home until 6 or
7 that night. "It makes for kind of a
long day," Margaret says.

On the map, Granville and East
Granville are only about eight miles
apart. Between them runs Braintree
Gap. In the summer, there's a road that
runs up over the mountain and con-
nects the two towns, but in this part of
Vermont summer doesn't last long and
the road closes when the snows come
in. Ever since anyone can remember
and for no very good reason that anyone can think of, East Granville has
been part of Granville.

Granville is an unprepossessing little
town with its backside in the Green
Mountains. There really isn't a main
street, unless Route 100, the skiers' free-
way, could be called a main street. The
houses sit right tight on the road and
seem to huddle together for protection.
In town, there's a general store, a wood-
en bowl mill, a clapboard mill, and a gas
station. There's also a one-room school-

*Even as a selectman, Gene Bagley gets
over to East Granville only twice a year.*

68

by Edie Clark • Photographs by Carole Allen

house where Granville's 13 elementary school students attend grades 1 through 6. (The children over in East Granville go to school in Randolph.)

Eula Bannister, known to most people in town as Mrs. Bannister, has taught these six grades for 19 years. Fully 80 percent of the town's budget is spent on the school. Mrs. Bannister lives down in Hancock, so she makes a point of not attending town meeting, when delicate issues of budget allocations are discussed, sometimes heatedly, by the town's taxpayers. "I want to give them a chance to fight out their differences without feeling they have to hold back because I'm there."

Town meeting is a time for settling differences, and it has been so for generations. In fact, the very subject of town meeting involves disagreement. Some say the meetings are a waste of time, a time when everything *but* town business gets talked about and a time when some people who attend just plain talk too much. Others, like Stanford Jarvis, say the meetings are vital, the only way town decisions can be made.

Gene Bagley is the chairman of Granville's board of selectmen. He lives only about an eighth of a mile from the Granville town hall, in a big white farmhouse that looks out over his cow barns. He says he doesn't get over to East Granville more than a cou-

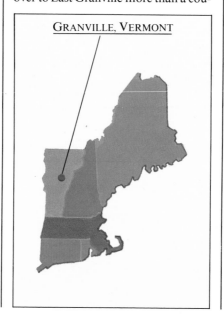

GRANVILLE, VERMONT

Along Route 100, the skiers' highway, homes in Lower Granville sit tight to the road (above). Eula Bannister, in back of her charges (right), runs the town's one-room schoolhouse.

ple of times a year, but nevertheless he feels it's very much a part of the town.

Overall, he characterizes Granville as "a quiet hill town. If you want excitement, you have to go out of town for that."

Maybe over to East Granville. Margaret Handly thinks her part of Granville has its own excitement. "We've got a cardinal staying here for the first time this winter, a coon we'd all like to get hold of, and, of course, there's Old Henry, who lives up on the hill." She laughs. "If we want a good time, we've got to make it ourselves."

Margaret Handly is a small, good-humored woman of 66 with lively eyes and lots of energy. She smokes tiny cigars and calls the people of East Granville "rocky people," referring, it would seem, to their grit. There are 18 houses in town and, if you stand in the right place, you can see just about all of

them in one glimpse. Margaret owns 12 of those 18 houses, which makes her the town's biggest landlord. She's the town's road agent and keeps the roads plowed in the winter, with either her jeep or her John Deere bulldozer. She takes a lot of pride in East Granville, and the fact that the town is somewhat of a stepchild seems to make it even more interesting to her.

Margaret can sit at her dining room table and count off the population of her town ("There's the Scotts, that's two, the Cooks are three more, and then the Curriers make nine . . .") and come up with an accurate headcount: 70 (that includes the two babies expected within the next two months), almost a quarter of Granville's total population of 284.

Back in the twenties, Margaret's father used to go over the mountain on snowshoes to get to the town meeting, stay overnight, and return the next day. "A lot more people went to town meeting in those days. And it was sure a lot harder to get there."

Four generations of Margaret's family have lived in East Granville, but none has ever lived over in Granville. "Granville's not exactly around the corner. It's around a lot of corners."

Gene Bagley puts it another way: "East Granville isn't so far away. It's just a lot of travel to get there."

– March 1982

Margaret Handly casts her vote. As the biggest landlord and road agent in East Granville, she always makes the 45-mile trip for town meeting. For a younger Granville resident (left) *the meeting can't possibly be over soon enough.*

Warren, Rhode

THE TOWN OF WARREN, Rhode Island, has been shaped by water. It is surrounded by two streams, the Kickamuit and the Warren, tidal rivers that slowly meander out to Narragansett Bay. The town faces the Warren but has depended upon both of them for its livelihood now for 350 years.

The town also has a beautiful beach, but don't expect to find many residents there on a bright Sunday afternoon. More than likely they will be back in the fields off Long Lane, playing softball and savoring the aroma of roasted quahogs at the Sunday clambakes. There are those who would call Warren the Clambake Capital, and anyone who has dined at one of these culinary extravaganzas would not be prone to argue.

Perhaps the bakes are distinctive because they have been going on now for more than 80 years. They were first begun by Warren's farmers to raise mon-

After more than 80 years at it, Warren has its weekly clambakes down to a science — Dave Harrison's antique fire engine (above) for kids, and lots of great eating (right) for grown-ups.

Island

by Bob Wyss • Photographs by David Witbeck

It's the volunteer firemen who stage the clambakes, stacking trays of clams, fish, onions, sweet and new potatoes, and corn on the steaming seaweed.

ey for the Kickamuit Grange. The grange still stands, but when the farmers tired of the feast in the 1930s, the town's six volunteer fire departments eagerly took over the task. "It has become a real family affair," observed Fire Chief John Conley, who supervises the six companies.

Up to 500 people, virtually all of them Warren residents, have been known to snap up all of the available tickets days in advance. The clams, flounder, onions, sweet potatoes, new potatoes, sausage, and dressing are roasted on hot stones, draped with seaweed, and covered with wet canvas. The knowledgeable come in the second half of August, when the native sweet corn is added.

The bake would not work if more people came. But Warren also would not be the same if it were any larger.

Warren is the smallest town in the smallest county in the smallest state. It is only 5.8 square miles in Bristol County, the tiniest of five counties in Rhode Island, a state that every schoolchild learns is no larger than a postage stamp.

And that's what residents like about Warren. "You can leave your car out on the street and not worry about locking it up," explained Charles Alfred, the town clerk who moved here from neighboring Bristol 20 years ago. "It's a place where you can walk on the water-

Dredging for oysters, once a lucrative occupation in Warren, was all but eliminated by hurricanes in 1938 and 1954.

– Courtesy Massasoit Historical Association

Down at Blount Seafoods on the Warren waterfront, a crane unloads quahogs harvested offshore. The clams seem to be making a comeback.

58,000 spindles.

Cheap labor was in demand, and soon Polish, Italian, Portuguese, French, and Irish immigrants were all crowding into Warren's waterfront tenements.

The mills went bust during the 1930s, but the town's economy was saved when firms such as American Tourister and Carol Cable moved into the rambling red brick edifices.

But times have been rougher down at the waterfront, particularly since the '38 and '54 hurricanes destroyed the oyster trade and hurt the quahogs. Only in the last few years have there been signs of a comeback.

Luther Blount is part of the reason. Blount began building wooden rowboats in the 1930s when he was still at Warren High School, and he now manages 100 craftsmen, who construct steel-hulled fishing trawlers and ferryboats inside the two steel warehouses at

front and not be scared."

The town was named for the British Admiral Sir Peter Warren, and it quickly grew into an important shipbuilding port. During most of the 18th and through the early 19th century, War- ren's docks were a haven for whalers and frigates that carried the slave trade. Then the textile mills arrived, particularly Warren Manufacturing Co., which was built on the north end to utilize the force of the tides to power

77

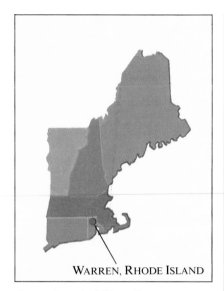

WARREN, RHODE ISLAND

the south end of Water Street.

Blount said he resisted opportunities to build in a more lucrative area. "Most of the people I hire worked before for my father and my grandfather, who had their own businesses down here," he said. "They would rather live here and work for less than to go farther away and make more money."

Today there is a growing pride in Warren and its heritage. It shows up on Water Street, where the antiques shops have begun replacing the bars. It is there in the Baker Street fire barn, which was restored three years ago to house the 1802 pumper called "Little Hero," one of the few still in existence. And it is to be found at the George Hail Free Library on Main Street, where residents recently contributed $250,000 to restore the interior.

"The thing I like about the town is the improvements in the old buildings that have taken place in the last ten years," said John Barry, who led the library restoration effort. "Walk down our streets and you find a feast, a veritable feast of 17th- and 18th-century homes."

"I never thought of going anywhere else," said Margaret White, who grew up here and lives in the house her grandfather erected in 1855. She can trace her roots back to Hugh Cole, one of the town's founders. "My children, however, were just the opposite. They could not wait to get out of here. But after a while, after a year or two, they were all ready to return."

– *August 1984*

78

Masts on sailboats moored in the tidal Warren River, one of two that define the town, share the skyline with the church steeples on the land.

Lake Winnipesaukee, New Hampshire

by Judson D. Hale, Sr. • Photographs by Joe Devenney

Tap Goodhue of Center Harbor took
advantage of a calm fall morning to
fly a remote-controlled model plane.

An unusually warm November day brings hardy sightseers for an excursion on the *Mt. Washington*.

URING THE SUMMER IT had been such a warm, cheerful, friendly lake, hosting thousands of boaters, campers, and swimmers. The shops and restaurants of its eight lakeside towns had been jammed with tourists, mostly from Massachusetts. Its historic old cruise ship, the M/S *Mount Washington,* recently extended to 230 feet in length, had carried up to 1,250 passengers on its daily summer rounds to Weirs Beach, Center Harbor, Alton Bay, and Wolfeboro. On warm summer nights, the *Mount* had meandered at half speed amongst some of the 274 islands, its lights blazing, the festive sounds of its orchestra drifting across the calm waters to summer cottagers viewing the evening from their porches and decks. "Smile of the Great Spirit" or "Beautiful Water in a High Place" is how the summer tourist brochures had translated the Indian word *Winnipesaukee.* Either one sounded right for New England's second-largest lake, the centerpiece of New Hampshire's popular Lakes Region.

But that was last summer. Now it is November. Most waterside restaurants and shops have been closed since the leaf spotters went home after Colum-

In season the Mt. Washington *leaves her Weirs Beach dock for daily tours; winters she's in Center Harbor.*

bus Day. The *Mount Washington* is tied up at its winter berth in Center Harbor. The summer cottagers have drained their water pipes, put their boats in storage, covered their chimneys to keep out squirrels and ducks (yes, ducks!), removed their porch screens, pulled up their swimming ladders, and returned to Massachusetts.

Left unto itself at last, "The Big Lake," as year-rounders call it, begins its mysterious, deep-water ritual all alone, just as it has been doing for thousands of Novembers. The surface water begins to cool, to contract and actually become heavier, eventually reaching the same density as the cold, dense, always-heavy bottom layer of water that remains about 39° Fahrenheit throughout the year, even in the summer.

Then come the great northwest winds, increasing in frequency and severity as the month progresses. Waves as high as eight or ten feet out in the 14-mile stretch of open water known as the "Broads" are not uncommon. After all, Winnipesaukee is only 40 air miles from Mount Washington (visible from the lake with its early snow cap), where the highest wind on earth was measured at 231 m.p.h. During a northwester in early December 1980, sustained winds of 145 m.p.h. streaked down the Broads for almost three hours.

These great winds now begin Winnipesaukee's seasonal "overturn," mixing the ever-denser surface water with the 39° water on which it has "floated" all summer. The hardy island cottagers who brave November weekends — curiously, the islanders are always the last to give up — notice that their drinking water, which still comes straight from the lake, suddenly tastes like mossy rocks. The bottom of Lake Winnipesaukee is coming to the top.

As the furious November winds and waves throw spray onto the windward sides of the islands, where the sturdy pine trees grow, the water freezes in the bushes and trees up to 15 feet high, save for the first foot or two above the lake's surface, which, though rapidly cooling, is still warm enough to melt it. On the lee sides, however, where the hardwoods grow, it's still foliage season! Foliage "peaks" on Winnipesaukee's islands as much as two weeks after the nearby mainland, which, in turn, peaks well after the surrounding mountain ranges. Summer flowers still bloom around island cottages long after frost has blackened their floral cousins on the mainland.

It's often said there are few "civilized days" on Winnipesaukee in November, but that is only a matter of opinion. John O'Connell, a former ocean sailor who left a New York ad agency career 15 years ago to buy and operate a marina in Wolfeboro, makes sure all the boats are stored away by November first — except for one of his own 23-foot sailboats. That one is kept in the water for his traditional Thanksgiving Day morning sail, foul weather (within reason!) or not.

"When the Broads are really churned up from a northwester," he says, "I like to look across the surface with binoculars and see the heat exchange taking place. It can be like a steaming cauldron out there!"

The lake has quiet times, too — but its deep-water November ritual continues uninterrupted. Thick fog, unlike any other time of the year, is the giveaway to what's happening below.

On these quiet days, one is surprised to see and hear the loons in Wolfeboro Bay. "Where did everybody go?" they seem to say as they swim and fly down from their usual nesting and living area far up the lake in Moultonboro. Through calm water one can see the smelt crowding near the shores and an occasional landlocked salmon streaking through them, mouth wide open.

This row of mailboxes on a beach road in Gilford (above) *testifies to the summer popularity of the lake. Season's end* (left) *means time to haul the boats for winter storage.*

Bay in Laconia. There's open water there all winter and people throw them French fries. Why bother flying south?

According to many lake people, natives as well as cottagers and tourists, the "human natural order of things" is beginning to go the way of the Burger King ducks.

"If you could express the biggest problem around here in a single word it would be *condos,*" says old-timer Harold Clough, owner of the West Alton Marina on the west shore below Glendale. "They come in here with bulldozers, chop down every tree right next to the lake . . . it makes you sick to see it." Harold shakes his head in disbelief.

Condominium developments have recently begun to seriously scar the natural beauty of Winnipesaukee. Some are on the water, some have only access to it, and others are back in the hills. With them are stores, gas stations, restaurants, all combining to create a glut of the human presence.

"At night, the mountains have lights on 'em now," laments Harold's wife,

The salmon are spawning in the brooks now, following the trout, who did their thing on the reefs and ledges a month or so earlier. An occasional deer is spotted swimming to one of the islands, perhaps instinctively knowing they are protected from November hunters on every Winnipesaukee island.

Although the lake is not on their usual flyway, geese are nonetheless sometimes seen flying extremely high over Winnipesaukee, heading south as their instinct compels. Winnipesaukee ducks, on the other hand, have found a new way to cope with their instincts and have recently become an exception to the natural order of things. To be sure, on some days they can be seen forming into groups on the lake *as if* in preparation for the trip south. But most are ultimately content to spend the winter at Burger King on Paugus

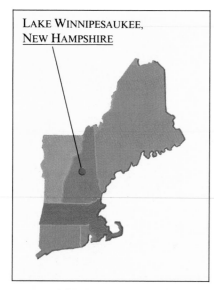

Ruth, adding that she often thinks it would be nice to move farther north where "today it's still like it was around *here* years ago."

Despite the growing concern (yes, even downright alarm), there seems to be no stopping the condominium developments. Says John O'Connell, now the manager of Wolfeboro's Corinthian Yacht Club, "These fellows appear before our local planning boards with a bunch of big-time city lawyers who first of all plunk down a stack of 'studies' — an ecological study, a forestry study, a water study, whatever — all of which supposedly prove their lake development plans conform with existing local town ordinances. Implicit in their presentations, too, is the threat that if the town won't allow them to proceed, they'll sue!"

And thus it is in New Hampshire's Lakes Region this month of November 1985. Somehow detached from the controversy raging around its 183 miles of shoreline, Lake Winnipesaukee, the Smile of the Great Spirit, continues mixing its water, replenishing itself from its hundreds of underground springs, refreshing and stirring itself with the northwest gales, simmering in the November fogs, and waiting. Waiting for its surface to freeze solid about the first week in January, when the ice fishing season and winter activities begin. Perhaps waiting, smiling, for the year when the ducks will fly south once again and human beings will know when to stop.   – *November 1985*

The lake gradually exhales its summer warmth in the form of fog, here wreathing a dock in Meredith.

Revere Beach, Massachusetts

by Tim Clark • Photographs by Chris Brown

Attractions like the Theatre Comique shown along The Boulevard in the postcard *(left)* made Revere Beach the place to be in 1906. Today, however, sitting along the seawall, watching the ocean *(below)* is fun enough.

Regulations required all "bathing costumes" be approved by the Park Commission in 1909. A different approval is usually sought nowadays.

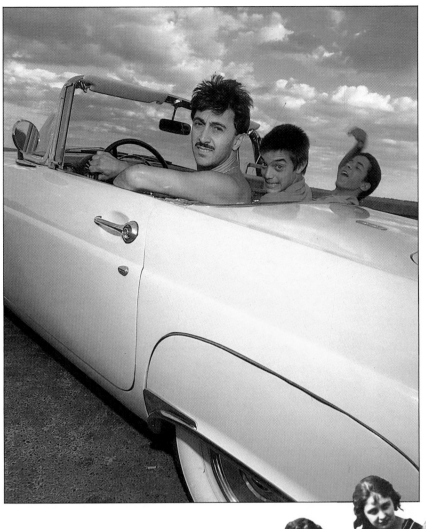

"IF I COULD GO BACK IN TIME," says Peter McCauley, unofficial historian of Revere Beach, Massachusetts, "I'd go back to 1908. There were six carousels then!"

Ladies in middy blouses and cambric skirts and men in straw hats. Sunday afternoon concerts in the bandstand. Fish dinners and saltwater taffy. McGinnis' Palace of Wonders and the Nautical Gardens, ten years before an August fire destroyed them. On the beach a 30-foot-high replica of Mount Vesuvius that belched real smoke. The Hippodrome, an electric carousel with five hand-carved wooden horses prancing abreast. Ice cream cones two for a nickel. A family place.

Only the bandstand remains, overlooking the three and a half miles of hard-packed sand that was and is the main everlasting attraction of the "Playground of New England." The last of the amusement parks was torn down in 1978 to make way for condos and apartments with an ocean view. "It's going to look like Miami," McCauley sighs.

When he was growing up in the late '20s and '30s, the genteel amusements

Although much of the honky-tonk flavor of the beach has faded, the frequent beauty pageants of old (below) *are mirrored in the brightly waxed fenders on display* (left).

91

Where once the famous
Hippodrome, with its
carved horses galloping
five abreast *(top left)*,
and a 30-foot replica
of Mount Vesuvius *(left)*
gave the city-weary an
exotic sense of escape,
all that remains is the
wrought-iron bandstand
in the background
and seawalls, where
relaxation is the byword.

In the '20s and '30s, Revere Beach put on a wilder face with the arrival of attractions like the death-defying Cyclone roller coaster (above).

of his parents' day were already changing, becoming louder and wilder. The Hippodrome and the Palace of Wonders gave way to the Thunderbolt, Lightning, Cyclone, and other roller coasters. McCauley's favorite was the Derby Racers, a parallel setup where the cars swooped around the rackety

tracks side by side, and everyone on the first car to finish won a free ride. "We knew the inside car didn't have as far to go; we always grabbed it. We left the outside car for the kids who were down from New Hampshire."

Revere Beach rose and fell with railroads and streetcars, McCauley says.

When a narrow-gauge steam railroad connected the beach with Boston in 1875, the working people had a way to escape the heat and turmoil of the city. Streetcars created suburbs, and suburbanites took the trolley to the shore. Bright-eyed barkers and shills invented diversions for the masses, the more pre-

posterous the better. There were dance halls and diving horses, fun houses and fireworks displays.

It was always a precarious business, though. "The season was so short," McCauley explains. "You had only ten weeks, twelve at the most. The rule of thumb was you had to make back your

rent and expenses by the Fourth of July or you were in trouble." Owners of the amusements got discouraged and moved south after a poor season or milked them for quick profits before selling out. The quality and safety of the rides and attractions declined, and for a while Revere Beach was not a

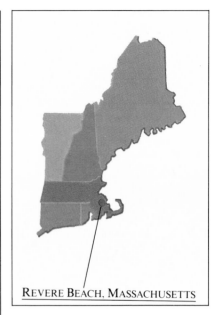

REVERE BEACH, MASSACHUSETTS

place to take the family. When automobiles became common after World War II, the working class looked elsewhere for summertime fun.

McCauley has spent the last 15 years collecting postcards and other reminders of Revere Beach's glory days, has published several books, and takes a slide show of old photographs around to show to those who remember what it was like. "People tell me, 'Don't make the show too long; old people get tired easily.' But when I try to stop after an hour or so, they won't let me. They see these pictures and they light up. They sparkle."

You can still ride the subway from Boston out to Revere Beach for a day in the sun, and thousands do, but it is quieter now; older folks and young parents with babies, dogs chasing Frisbees into the surf, joggers tuned in to the private rhythms of their earphones. If someone from 1908 could visit Revere Beach today, he might find its atmosphere not so different; you don't need a permit to wear a bathing costume anymore, but it is once again a family place. What's missing is the music; the wheezing of the calliope, the dignified oompah of the Sunday concerts, and the stately mechanical waltz of the carousels.

"There's an old carousel out in western Massachusetts that the state owns," says McCauley. "We're trying to get it. It's just not Revere Beach without a carousel." *– August 1985*

Danville, Vermont

by Howard Frank Mosher • Photographs by Stephen O. Muskie

"WHATEVER YOU DO, don't call it the common," Dick Peterson told me good-naturedly. "I made the same mistake when I first came here. It's the Danville green."

Standing in front of Dick's big red general store and looking across U.S. Route 2 at the four-acre park around which most of Danville is arranged, I was impressed — regardless of the local nomenclature. From Dick's corner we could see the Caledonia National Bank (one of the oldest independent banks in Vermont), the tiny white post office, the village library, the high school, the town hall, the Methodist and Congregational churches, and perhaps half of the well-kept old houses in this northern Vermont community of about 600. Situated on a lofty plateau overlooking the Presidential Range of New Hampshire to the east and the northern extension of Vermont's Green Mountains to the west, the village of Danville is a pretty sight to see.

Actually, it isn't surprising that residents are particular about what you call their green with its tall maples, wood-and-brick bandstand, and granite monument to local men "who victoriously defended the Union during the War of Rebellion." George Webster, whose ancestors helped found Danville in the late 18th century, told me some of its history. "The green was deeded to the town by two original settlers as a site for the courthouse and jail. But in 1855, the county seat was moved to St. Johnsbury, and this may have been the best thing that ever happened to Danville. Instead of evolving into a center of administration with people coming and going constantly, the village has been able to retain its distinctive character as a village."

There's no doubt about it. For nearly two centuries, the people of Danville have staunchly preserved the continuity and independence of their home around the green. Dick Peterson calls it the most dynamic town of its size in Vermont, and it may be just that. On Mother's Day the fire department hosts

Heather Wightman lugs a bale of hay to her Dorset sheep on her family's 25-acre Windswept Farm on Webster Hill Road, just outside of town.

97

Eileen and Dick Peterson own the general store on the edge of the Danville Green. They came here after teaching school for 27 years in Massachusetts and Connecticut.

DANVILLE, VERMONT

The view from Walden Hill Road takes in the Methodist Church and the Presidential Range.

its annual turkey or ham dinner. In July it's the Catholic Church's barbecue. Throughout the summer there are weekend flea markets, open-air band concerts and recitals, pick-up ball games, and, on the second Wednesday in August, the Danville Fair, featuring traditional local products like maple sugar, honey, and handmade quilts, as

well as old-fashioned events like horse pulling. Later, near the peak of the fall foliage season, thousands of visitors arrive for the yearly convention of the American Society of Dowsers, whose headquarters is located on the south edge of the village. And just before snow flies, the Methodists put on an abundant wild game dinner.

Danville has maintained its integrity as a village in other ways as well. Two years ago, the fire and rescue unit considered going after federal assistance for a new building. Outside consultants estimated that it would cost about $300,000. So much for that option. Eschewing government money (and advice), the village decided to go it alone.

With volunteer labor and donated supplies, the total cost of a new building was about $40,000. A decade or so earlier, the village school could have become part of a larger, consolidated union. Danville citizens were more than proud of their existing school system, thank you anyway, supported it generously, and saw no advantage in a merger. Rodger Boyle, the native-born principal, told me that the high school has recently added courses in economics and computer technology, but still offers three full years of Latin and a first-rate agricultural program with a stable enrollment. And both Mr. Boyle and Catherine Beattie, whose 60-cow dairy farm has been in her family for nearly 150 years, say there's a strong commitment on the part of local young people to keep the remaining farms in town going.

Not that the people I talked with seemed opposed to change. It's just that they intend to change things in their own way. In 1977, for example, Danville residents got together and es-

tablished a modern health clinic, which served 2,600 clients last year. Former cow pastures on the edge of town have been converted into attractive rural homesites for people who work in St. Johnsbury and Lyndonville; and although the grand old Eagle Hotel on the green burned in 1889, and the 17 potato-whiskey mills along Joe's Brook and the Sleeper River have long since distilled themselves into fumy memories, George Webster and a committee of 50 or so other people are planning a Danville town history, which has never been written.

Even Ida Woods, at 83, has made some changes recently. Twenty years ago, when her husband died, Mrs. Woods found herself alone on their small hilltop farm with 100 bushels of potatoes ready to be harvested. "I went outside and looked at the tractor," she told me. "I'd never driven it, or anything else but a horse. I was scared to death, but I got on and somehow I got it started. Well, mister, I dug and drew 12

bushels of potatoes that day. A week later, I had all 100 bushels sorted and sold. I've sold vegetables for my living ever since. But last year I got disgusted

Foster Page (above), *of Hill St., takes Jack and Billy for a spin. Cabinet-maker Gene Nunn* (left) *was born down the road in Peacham. Ida Woods* (right) *never learned to drive a car but manages to run her truck farm from the seat of her tractor.*

with sending them out on commission and getting only 25 percent. I made a decision."

I waited for Ida Woods to tell me she'd planted her last garden. Instead she said, "I decided to set up a stand right here on the corner of my road. It was the best season ever. In one day I sold 100 cukes."

Toward the end of our conversation, I asked Mrs. Woods what she liked best about living in Danville. She looked out her kitchen window over the village and farms below and mountains beyond. Then she smiled. "You know, now that I think of it, there isn't anything that I *don't* like about living here." *– April 1984*

Whately, Massachusetts

IN WHATELY, THE CONNECTICUT River borders the east edge of town, and the strawberries and raspberries and asparagus are planted right to the river's edge. The east side is where the tobacco farms were, the farms with fields as flat as Kansas, divided up by the long, windowless tobacco barns. A town of 1,300, Whately remains solidly inside two, maybe three centuries, keeping the stately main street with the fine old homes and the double row of maples a safe distance from the Castaway Lounge, where women, and sometimes men, are hired to dance nude to music from a jukebox.

A little, out-of-the-way town a lot of people call it, and there's not a lot to refute that. In town there's just the post office, a town hall, the inn, and, on a hot summer's day, the smell of fresh-cut hay. But the town has always had access. There are five colleges within ten miles of Whately, and one of them, the University of Massachusetts campus at Amherst, can be seen down across the wide open fields from many people's windows. The Boston and Maine railroad runs through town, which is four miles wide and six miles long, and so does Interstate 91. On the north side is an all-night diner, where truckers from Quebec or Nebraska can fill up on items from a lengthy menu, perhaps the Heavy Hauler's Special with a side of baked beans and brown bread. All that access made it easy to move the premium cigar tobacco that made Whately rich among its neighbors, but it also brought the rest of the world with it.

The Castaway, a squat building made of cinder blocks and painted yellow, is at the edge of one of the old tobacco fields. It used to be just a bar but the traffic coming through wasn't thirsty enough so the owner brought in some entertainment, what was called exotic dancing, something the people living

John Kennedy has handled oxen since he was 10, buying and selling teams. "I'm not married to any of them."

by Edie Clark • Photographs by Shelley Rotner

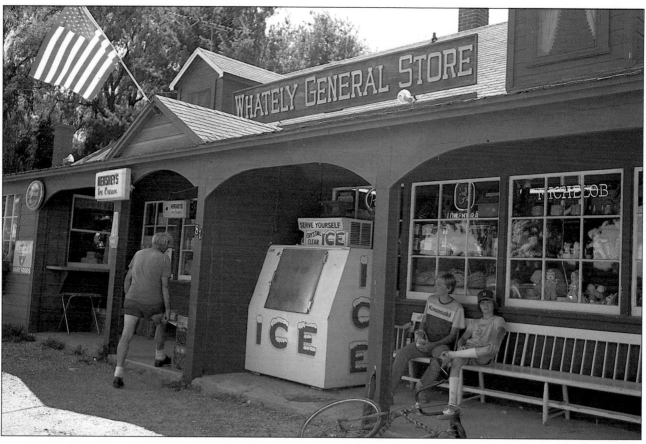

nearby found shocking.

"The people didn't feel that Whately was the kind of place for that kind of entertainment. Springfield, yes, but a town this size, that's another thing. It went back and forth, there were lawsuits filed by the town, but we weren't able to close them down," Fred Bardwell, a Whately selectman, said recently. The debates about whether or not a town like Whately should have nude dancing, when practically the only other enterprise in town was a general store, went on for about seven years. While the selectmen and the elders of the town fumed, the dancers kept on dancing and the rest of the town kept on talking. There were those who called it "disgusting" and "out of character," but it began to seem that just as many were finding it, as one woman said, "fascinating."

"It was finally put to a popular vote at the regular town meeting. It was a close vote, but the town voted for it,

The only store in town, the Whately General Store sells the essentials, as well as souvenirs and hardware.

215 to 196. So the issue is not a closed book," Bardwell said.

Which left Whately with exotic entertainment they couldn't drive away and without the tobacco they couldn't beg to stay.

The tobacco through the years has played a fickle game with the town. It thrived through the 1700s and the early 1800s, but in 1855 the profits dropped and wiped out most of the farmers in town. By 1900 it was back, and, according to the Whately town history, as the century progressed there was scarcely a farmer who didn't put in at least an acre of Havana broadleaf or a few acres of shade-grown Sumatra. By the fifties, however, tobacco companies had begun the practice of homogenizing, which is a way of mixing all the grades of tobaccos, controlling the fla-

vor through sweeteners. This process made the distinctive and superior Whately leaf no longer special. Once again tobacco slumped, but in the seventies it looked as if it were coming back again. That rise was only temporary, and today there are only four farmers in town who plant tobacco.

Since tobacco had more or less left, market gardeners, some of them the same farmers who once haggled with tobacco buyers, now grow lettuce, tomatoes, apples, cauliflower, celery, peaches, corn, broccoli, rhubarb, horseradish, cucumbers, squash, onions, potatoes, and a wide selection of Chinese vegetables. Some of these fields are open to the public for picking. There are also a number of farmstands by the side of the road, selling produce that's just been picked. The vegetables

Growing tobacco once supported the town — even teenagers were hired to sort leaves. There's little left today.

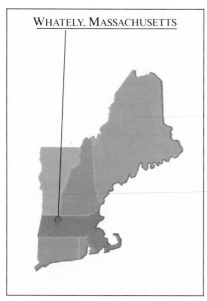

grow so prolifically in this river bottom soil that even the townspeople, if they have a few extra vegetables from their backyard gardens, set them out on their lawns, naming their prices on hand-lettered signs. Louis Kandsz, a distributor of seed potatoes and onions based in Whately, is one who thinks the exodus of the tobacco industry was a good thing. "The tobacco companies took over and tried to run this valley. It ruined the 'little' farmer. One thing we don't want now is tobacco."

But unfortunately this isn't a matter about which the town can vote. They can only speculate.

John Kennedy, who has raised tobacco nearly all of this century, has most recently had potatoes and corn in his fields where there always was tobacco. "I would have mortgaged the farm and bet all the money that there would *always* be tobacco in this valley. I think the problem is that people can't stand the price of a good cigar."

David Scott, along with his father, continues to raise tobacco as the family has for generations. On five acres of their dairy farm, they raise Connecticut broadleaf. "Tobacco's a funny business. Some years there are buyers around and you can pretty much name your price. Other years it's hard to sell. But it's like anything else. If you raise a good crop and take care of it right, there'll be someone there to buy it. Tobacco's gonna come back, I'm certain of that." — *June 1984*

Aerial view of the Whately section of the River Road shows the fine level fields of rich alluvial loam.

by Mel Allen • Photographs by Carole Allen

Williamstown

"**It drew** *to the village all the people of the countryside, and there were booths for gingerbread and root beer, and sellers of whips and toy balloons. . . . Few of the hundreds of country people who flocked to the show paid much attention to the graduation exercises.*"

– RECOLLECTIONS BY WASHINGTON GLADDENS DESCRIBING HIS COMMENCEMENT FROM WILLIAMS COLLEGE IN 1856.

THE COLLEGE AND ITS town: They share a common father, Ephraim Williams, who died in a French and Indian ambush on September 8, 1755. A lover of literature, he provided in his will for a "free school" in the frontier settlement of West Hoosac if the settlers would rename it Williamstown. They did so in 1765 when Williamstown was incorporated. Not until October 1793 did Williams College open with "18 gangling farm youths" and two teachers, making it the second oldest college in Massachu-

In his 1755 will Ephraim Williams (above) *provided money to rename a town and found a college* (right).

Massachusetts

Old-fashioned pie-eating contests and the like are among the mainstays of the Williamstown Grange Agricultural Fair each September.

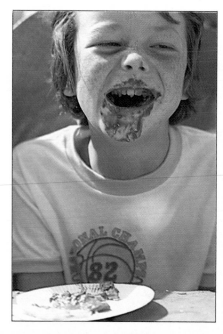

More than 60 years old, the fair offers all the traditional trappings of a good agricultural fair: competitions in everything from sewing and canning to poultry and livestock judging, always of interest to farmers (left). The college community brings its own touch to the fair with unusual offerings like juggling classes (above).

setts. Ever since, the town and the college have been connected, yet apart — each a world unto itself, yet each inseparable from the other. Each treats the other with respect tinged with caution, an odd brew of love and loyalty, envy and suspicion. Conservative farmers, liberal college, still wary of an ambush.

In spite of its beauty, its tourism, its famed art museum and summer theater, Williamstown remains a college town. "If we could pick up the college and take it away, Williamstown could not survive," admits town manager Howard Redfern. If the college were a mill, Williamstown would be called a company town (except this mill pays few taxes) and a very anxious one, were anything to threaten the mill. Fortunately, Williams is one of a handful of small colleges that seem secure in the face of declining enrollments, turning away eight applicants for every acceptance. With 700 employees and 1,200 townspeople whose livelihoods are tied to the college, roughly $20 million is pumped into the economy of this rural, farm-based town that historically has had only minimal industry. Even with a surge of wealthy retirees into town, a quarter of the people are dependent on the college. One man said, "Some feel the college is untouchable, so they resent it."

At the best of times the town and gown are friends. At commencement the homes of townspeople are opened to the families of graduates. During the year town children romp in the end zone during football games, shoot baskets with the basketball players, covet the broken sticks of the hockey players. "You'd think the sticks were gold," a woman says. They swim in the pool, study in the library, and attend free recitals. Bill Paradise, who owns the Williams News Shop, grew up in the fifties behind the fraternities that later were abolished. "I grew up with all the boys," he says. "I wasn't pleased when it went coeducational. I molded myself after them. I wore chinos, tucked-in shirts, and striped ties to high school. I still dress like they do — or used to." One woman today calls it "Camp Williams." But still, they are not family. They can wear sweatshirts in the school color, purple, but they are not *blood*.

Behind the library, facing the tennis courts, lies a cemetery reserved for trustees and professors and, until they became too numerous, alumni. *This* is for family.

In a small town (Williamstown has 6,700 residents plus 2,000 college students) the distinctions often blur. The municipal building is housed in a former fraternity house, "probably the only town hall with a bar in the basement," an official says.

"One criterion for getting tenure was community involvement," says a former dean. "It wasn't written down, but teachers knew it."

Three of the last four chairmen of the school board have been Williams faculty; and the excellence of the public schools — three of four graduates from the regional high school go on to college — is used to lure faculty to Williams. The publisher of the town newspaper is a former dean of freshmen; the editor is the wife of a professor. The college uses the town's quiet gracefulness and magnificent scenery to recruit. "We're told it's worth money in our

A mother's opening-day good-bye.

paycheck to be able to live here," says a professor ruefully.

Williamstown is tucked into the northwest pocket of Berkshire County, spreading along the narrow valleys cut by the Green River and Hemlock Brook. Its woods are thick with deer and pheasant, cows graze on pastures that roll off into the hills, and its back roads dip and curve past ravines with names that resonate with the days of isolation: Treadwell Hollow, Young's Hollow, Mill's Hollow, Fowler's Vale, Kidder Pass.

To the west lies New York State, to the north Vermont, and all around, as far as one can see, are the mountains.

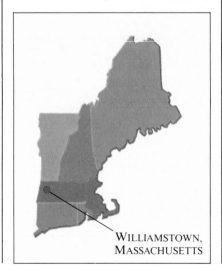

WILLIAMSTOWN, MASSACHUSETTS

Williamstown may indeed be, as its citizens say, the most beautiful town in the state. Long ago Hawthorne looked down on Williamstown from a mountain: "It was like a daydream," he wrote.

But for a long time, until the railroad poked its way west through the Hoosac Tunnel, the ruggedness of Williamstown was a nightmare for the young college. "There has run through the history of Williamstown . . . a sometimes open, sometimes unspoken wish that the college might physically remove itself from the town," wrote Charles F. Rudolph, a Williams College historian. Students lamented that they were marooned in a "wilderness without even a stagecoach to connect it with the outside world." In 1821, certain the college would fail, the Williams president, Zephaniah Swift Moore, took his best students and trekked over the mountains to found Amherst College — thus beginning a legendary rivalry. Amherst remains the one team Williams must defeat.

Every time the college came close to failure, the townspeople, mostly rugged farm folk, held lotteries to keep it going. And gradually its reputation and its campus grew. The first alumni association in America began here, and Williams became known for the fierce loyalty of its graduates. President James A. Garfield, Class of 1856, was en route to Williams to attend his 25th reunion when he was shot in a train station in Washington.

In time, the students grew to love the mountains, as long as they could leave them from time to time. A day each autumn was declared "Mountain Day," when students and faculty tramped together to nearby peaks. (It's been 50 years since the last "Mountain Day," however.) Thoreau, upon visiting the college, was moved to write, "Some will remember, no doubt, not only that they went to college, but that they went to the mountain."

And each September the ritual repeats. The beginning of memories of burning leaves and bell chimes, of the single strip of shops, of mountains and friends. And one day, years later, they will return, pulled by a love of place they cannot define except to know it is far more elusive than stone and brick.
– September 1983

On opening day, Williams College students attend the Purple Key fair to sign up for clubs and activities.

◆Millinocket◆

Y OU HAD ONLY TO LOOK out the window of any house, office, or store on Main Street in East Millinocket. There was the steaming mill with its ring of freight cars, its gray mountains of bark and logs. In Millinocket, the white lights on those giant chimneys would flash at you on the densest, darkest, rainiest day.

Before the mills there had been no towns. Eighty years ago, it had been the forest and the river, but mainly the river — the West Branch of the Penobscot — that had lured the paper company into the wilderness. The river's steep descent from Ripogenus Lake meant power for machines downstream — machines to turn spruce and fir into paper.

The mountain rose above the dark forest and the mills as if it were the moon, its face old and fearsome, but the young couple did not seem to notice. They were going shopping. Mount Katahdin was theirs in the sense that this place was their home. Yet I was the one who pointed it out: "There it is."

They did not say anything. By the time we drove into the forest on the other side of the causeway you could not see the mountain any more.

After a while I leaned forward in the back seat. "Have you ever been there, to the mountain?" I asked.

"Once," Fred said. "When I was in the eighth grade. The whole class went."

"I like the beach," his wife said.

I sat back and looked out the window into the woods. I supposed Fred's wife would not especially like the mountain or want to go to it because she was a girl from a big city and the mountain was a part of the small place in the Maine wilderness in which, I sensed, she felt herself confined.

Her name was Ho-Ja and she was from Korea. Fred Moore, Jr., a wood poler at the East Millinocket mill, had met her in Seoul when he was in the

Maine

by Willis Johnson
Photographs by Stephen O. Muskie

New emission standards have helped
towns like Millinocket reduce the
amount of sulfur dioxide in the air.

Marines. They lived in a new house on Independence Lane, the newest street in East Millinocket.

It was a nice house with a good dry cellar that Fred was filling with firewood for the winter. His mortgage payments were over $400 a month, but he was making good money poling wood, and he could pay that and all the other bills and still put $500 a month in the bank.

"Sometimes more," Ho-Ja said.

Fred was a short man with a broad, open face, wide-set eyes, and a reddish blond beard. He had come off the overnight shift at eight that morning and he hadn't slept. His eyes were red and you could see he was tired, but he had the next two days off and he said he didn't like to waste the first one sleeping.

He was only 27 but he already had his retirement figured out. In 2002 he'd have his 30 years in. He'd be 49, Ho-Ja 47. With their savings and his pension from the mill they could go live in Korea. Or maybe they would move to Washington, D.C., or someplace like that where they could buy a business.

It was kind of a tradition, the mill. His father worked there, and his brother Rick. So had his grandfather. It was that way with a lot of families in town.

And the work had always been shift work; you got used to it. It wasn't as if everyone else had their evenings and their weekends free. Most everyone in town was on a schedule. So it wasn't so bad.

Of course it wasn't easy, either, poling wood eight hours a day with only a single 20-minute break. The logs came in four-foot lengths up the conveyor belt from the wood room and dropped into the tank. You pulled them out of the black water of the tank with your pick pole and pushed them through the troughs to the grinders to be ground into pulp. Your hands blistered, you pulled the muscles in your back and arms, and sometimes the grindermen would jab themselves with their picaroons. In the tank it was freezing in the winter, and over the grinders the steam came boiling up as if the grindermen were feeding those logs down into hell. And that's what went on in the mills 24 hours a day, seven days a week, pulling and grinding a million cords of wood a year with only a break for lunch.

"One of the bosses said to me once,

'We're giving away money in the grinding room.' " Fred gave a laugh. "They ain't giving away a thing." he said. "That money, it's all earned."

Fred had bought his house lot from Great Northern, which was what you had to do if you wanted to build a house, because the paper company owned all the land, two million acres and more. You had to apply, and when the company had enough people on its list for a new street, it would tell the town and the town would put in the road and the water line.

Fred Moore was told by the company the kind of house he had to build on his lot, how much it had to cost, how far back it needed to be set, the date by which it had to be up, and when he had to have his lawn in. And Fred was happy because the new house meant more space. He and Ho-Ja and their year-old daughter Susan Marie had been living in an apartment in town and Ho-Ja was pregnant again.

Ho-Ja told me that Fred's brother Rick had recently married her best friend in Korea. Ho-Ja had given him her address. They had been writing for some time, and last summer Rick went over to Seoul and married her. He was home now, and his wife Yung was going to follow him soon.

Ho-Ja remembered the day she had come to America. She had flown into Bangor. Fred had not been able to get home from Camp LeJeune, and his father and mother had met her at the airport in their pickup truck.

As she drove north with her new in-laws, the cars on the road grew fewer and fewer, and after Lincoln and Mattawamkeag, some of the towns on the road signs had numbers instead of names. And all she saw were the woods. "I didn't know where I was going," she said.

Two days later she was in her room at her in-laws' in East Millinocket when Fred's mother called, "Ho-Ja, there's someone here to see you." She came out, and there at the foot of the stairs was Fred. She sat on the top stair and cried.

The next summer Fred was discharged. Ho-Ja had moved in with a Korean family outside Washington so she could be nearer Camp LeJeune. She liked it there, but Fred wanted to return home.

"I had it planned I was going to come back here and get my job back," he said.

We stopped at the shopping center for groceries, and since it was noon we went to a restaurant for lunch. Ho-Ja and Fred went up to the buffet table for dessert, and as I waited it struck me that I rarely heard anyone in the two towns talk about the mountain. People talked about their camps and their snowmobiles, they talked about the deer they hunted and the foremen they hated. They spoke of paper machines as if they were prominent or notorious citizens of the town. Over and over I heard the names of the machines — Number Five, Number Nine — but I never heard anyone say Katahdin.

Except Wiggie Robinson. His name was Wilmot, but I never heard anyone call him that. He would say, "Katahdin is just brilliant today."

Every morning when he came out his front door he saw it if the weather was clear. He would look down that old road in the direction of the new development and, where the road dipped down the hill into Millinocket, he would see the mountain. Then he would go back in the house and tell Joyce the way it looked.

Wiggie was out of the mill as much as anyone. From fifth hand on Number Five paper machine to machine tender and finally foreman on Numbers Four, Five, and Six paper machines, he had given 34 years to the mill. And his son.

Wiggie was also of the mountain and the forest. He was a small man with only as much weight to him as he needed. His nose was sharp, and in his eyes was the look of a hawk.

One morning Wiggie took me for a closer look at Katahdin. He had just retired from Great Northern. He had plenty to do with looking after his bird dogs, carting eight cords of wood into the cellar, and writing a column about the out-of-doors for the local newspaper, but now it was his time, no longer the company's time, and he could take a break when he wanted.

It was a cold, clear morning. We drove out the Golden Road, the road Great Northern has built into its forests to the north and west of Millinocket. It is a private road, straighter and better than the public road that parallels it as far as Baxter State Park, where the

mountain is, but you can use it so long as you move over for the trucks that haul in the tree-length logs from the cutting areas.

Some logs the trucks take directly to the mills, and some they pile along the road to use in the mud season in the spring, when the machines can't get into the woods to get the trees out. The logs on the roadside were piled 15 or 20 feet high, and driving down that road between them was like driving through a canyon. The air was filled with the scent of the pine logs.

Wiggie had been coming into these woods all his life. When he was 11, he spent a summer at Chimney Pond, sleeping on a bedding of boughs, smelling their fragrance, climbing the mountain and exploring the forest. When he was a young man he got his guide's license. He paddled fishermen around, took hunters through the woods and saw they didn't get lost. He built their fires, boiled the kettle, helped them get what they were after. And it was a thing he loved to do, being out like that, but you could never make as much at it as you could make in the mill.

Wiggie had resisted going into the

Fred Moore, Jr., with his wife Ho-Ja and their daughter Susan Marie (left). In the grinding room of the mill (above), Fred poles four-foot pulp logs out of the tank and feeds them into the roaring grinders that each year reduce one million cords of wood into chips for pulp. In winter, steam can come boiling up out of the grinders so that grindermen feel like they're feeding the logs down into hell. Grindermen, says Fred, earn every penny they're paid.

117

The Golden Road, part of a network of unpaved roads built and maintained by the paper company, is the pipeline that keeps the logs flowing to the mill.

mill until the year he got married, 1946. He was 24 years old, home from the war. He had been a truck driver and a meat cutter before the war. When he came home he had done a little carpentry and construction work for Joyce's father. In the winter, when the building work slowed down, Wiggie went to the mill superintendent and asked what the chances were of getting into the machine shop where his father had worked before he died. The superintendent advised him to go into the paper room because that was where the money was, and the advancement.

A paper machine is a huge machine, maybe 80 or 100 yards long, and to work on it is to work in great heat and in great noise. Your sweat soaks your clothes, and if you want to talk to someone you must put your face close to his and shout in his ear. Wiggie started on such a machine as the bottom man of a five-man crew, at $34.65 a week. When he retired 34 years later he was still in the paper room with the heat and the noise, a little deaf and making over $30,000 a year. All of his four children followed him into the mill, the girls working in the office, the boys in the paper room, until Michael was killed on Number Ten. After that, Jason, Wiggie's younger son, became a

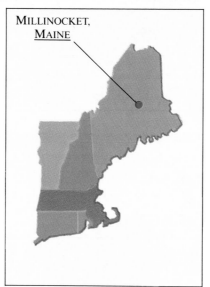

MILLINOCKET, MAINE

swiper, cleaning up in the pits below the great machines.

We came to a place on the Golden Road where a machine was lifting logs from a truck and stacking them on the roadside. The machine was maneuvering in the road and we had to stop and wait. The sun was in our laps as we waited, and we watched the machine and the man in it, who waved to us. The blue sky was fringed with the dark tops of the trees. And Wiggie said how he loved this country, the forest and the mountain, how he had been around the world in the Army and had been down to Florida, but he wouldn't live anywhere else.

Just 25 miles away, Mt. Katahdin rises over Millinocket. Great Northern owns 5,000 of the 7,000 acres that comprise the town.

Then he began to talk about Michael. It was as if the boy had been so naturally a part of this place, of the forest, the sky, the mountain, the smell of the spruce and fir, that Wiggie could not talk about it without including him.

"He could fly-fish, he could wing-shoot . . . he learned with hardly any teaching. He shot his first deer when he was 11 — imagine, 11 years old.

"We were rabbit hunting with 20-gauge shotguns," Wiggie said. His voice had dropped down, quiet, as if he were again in the woods with the boy. "I heard a bang. Then I heard, 'Dad! Dad!' I went over and he had shot a doe and he was sitting on her. He was afraid she might get up and run away. He helped me dress her out. He had got her with a shoulder shot — a running deer.

"Mike didn't want to go to work in the mill right off like other kids do when they get out of high school — they want to go into the mill and start earning that good money. Instead, when he was 19 he went with a trapper and spent the whole winter living in the woods, trapping one place, then moving on to another — beaver, foxes, pine martin."

The machine took the last log from the truck and laid it on top of the canyon wall. Then it pulled off to one side and we drove past and the operator waved at us again.

We drove to Wiggie's camp on the West Branch. Wiggie started a fire in the stove and put on the coffeepot. I went onto the porch to look at the river and the mountain with its shawl of snow, radiant in the blue sky.

Wiggie and Joyce had bought the camp a few months earlier. It was on paper company land, as were all the camps on all these lakes and rivers, but Wiggie didn't have to pay the company the $160 a year rent for the lot it was on, because he was a retired Great Northern employee.

Wiggie put out two cups. Joyce was coming out from town with lunch, and we had a little while to wait. Wiggie wrapped his hands around his coffee cup to keep them warm.

Michael, he told me, finally had gone into the mill sometime after he turned 20, starting as a fifth hand in the paper room, as his father had, because that's

Retired from the mill after 34 years, Wiggie Robinson spends time at his camp on the West Branch. On the bottom of 1938 photo of himself and Joyce Morgan (left), *he notes, "This is the gal I married in 1946."*

where the money was, and the advancement. The next year, in 1974, he got married. The next year he was dead.

He had been on Number Ten paper machine. The levelator had risen from the floor to take off a roll of paper. Michael was in between working on the paper, and the hydraulic arm of the levelator came down and crushed him.

Wiggie was up by Number Five. There was a commotion, and someone ran past with a stretcher. Wiggie ran then.

"They tried to hold me back. When they did, I knew it was my son."

After they buried Michael, people came to him and said, "You ought to sue them, Wiggie. Something had to have gone wrong for the levelator arm to come down on him like that."

"Why didn't you?" I asked.

"What good would it do?" Wiggie asked. "I might get some money, but what is that? I still had to work in the mill. I still had to live in the town. I couldn't change my life."

AS A WOOD POLER, FRED MOORE, Jr. had made a common laborer's wage, the lowest in the mill. After high school he had worked in the mill for a few weeks and then had gone into the Marines. After the Marines he had gone straight into the mill, so he was one of those 70 percent of local graduates the high school counselors lamented about, the ones who didn't bother with "broadening their horizons."

Last year, with overtime, Fred made more than $29,000. There was not a guidance counselor nor a teacher, nor anyone else in the entire East Millinocket and Millinocket school systems who made so much. Most of them didn't make half that, with all their college degrees.

There were a lot of benefits besides the salary and the fringes and the fact that he could retire with a good pension before he was 50. If he wanted firewood, for instance, Great Northern would let him cut it on its land for six dollars a cord. If he needed scrap lumber, he could buy a whole truckload from Great Northern for a dollar. The chemical drums Fred had brought home for trash cans, the matting he had laid over their driveway so they wouldn't get their feet muddy — it all had come from the mill.

There was a time when the company would even pour your foundation for you. It didn't do that anymore. It had changed since it merged with some oth-

er companies and made a bigger one they called Great Northern Nekoosa, which had its headquarters down in Stamford, Connecticut. Not long ago, the town of East Millinocket didn't make you pay taxes if you were on social security or you were retired or a widow or disabled somehow. The mill, which was paying something like 80 percent of the town taxes, went along with it. That had changed, too. The company started complaining, and pretty soon everybody's property taxes went up and the mill's went down.

Still, the mill was generous in other ways. It gave money to the music boosters, the Boy Scouts, the hockey league, and to all kinds of charities; it even helped the local country club with its expenses. Once it gave $400,000 to the Millinocket hospital.

If you started feeling sorry for yourself, you just had to take a ride around and look at other places. In a lot of places in Maine people live in shacks with junk all around their yards and there isn't any work, let alone a minimum of $7.78 an hour in the mill, which goes to $8.13 for the overnight shift, and you get double time whenever you work a Sunday, which happens three times a month.

One morning I dropped by Wiggie's house on the old Medway Road. He had gone out, Joyce said. "Come see what's out back."

She led me through the kitchen to the garage, where a deer was hanging from a bar and chain. There was a cardboard box under its nose to catch the blood.

"It's a big one," I said tentatively.

"Isn't he pretty?" Joyce asked.

Wiggie had shot him that weekend. He was going to take him to the general store in Benedicta, where they were having a contest. Wiggie had shot bigger ones in his time, and this deer probably would not win. He had cut out the heart and liver because he had shot the deer four miles in and had to leave it overnight. At first he was not going to kill the deer because he was so far in. But the deer had stepped into a little clearing and stopped there, sniffing the air. Wiggie wasn't going to take him, and he said that to the deer. You and I are just too far in, my friend, but he lowered on him anyhow. And then through his scope he saw that rack, that

lovely rack.

The next day I went with Wiggie to weigh the deer. He had borrowed his son-in-law's pickup; the deer was in the back with the iron bar through its legs. We followed the Grindstone Road along the East Branch of the Penobscot. After a while the land began to open up with a farm here and there. That meant we were out of the paper company's land.

On the way, Wiggie wanted to show me a place he had thought about buying. It was a house with a good bit of acreage. His lot in Millinocket was 50 by 100 feet, like the rest of the older lots in town, and he thought it would be nice to have some land for his bird dogs and for himself. He had talked it over with Joyce, and they had decided against it. It was not easy to leave a house you had lived in for more than 30 years, a house where you'd raised your four children.

"It's up ahead," Wiggie said. "Gosh, it looks like it's still for sale." We passed it. It looked like a nice place.

"I guess it wasn't meant to be." Wiggie shrugged. He thought a minute and said, "You know how sometimes you think there is something you really want to have or to do, and then for one reason or another you don't do it? You go this way instead of that? It's amazing to me how often it turns out that what you did or didn't do was the right thing. You know what I mean? It makes you believe in fate, as though things are assigned."

We came to the store. The weather was turning warmer. The sky was fading out. Wiggie backed the truck up to the scales. The owner came out of the store, pulled down the hoist, and hooked it onto the bar that went through the deer's legs. Then he winched it up.

He climbed a stepladder to read the scale. "Hundred ninety pounds," he said.

That night we were going to a bean supper at the Millinocket Baptist Church. When Wiggie got in my car he said that with this weather he'd have to butcher the deer tomorrow or the next day. The supper was in the church basement. Only men were there. Most of them worked in the mill or were retired from the mill, and they talked close to one another's faces, as if they still need-

ed to be heard over the roar of the machines. The cooks served up beans and brown bread and hot dogs.

After the supper they had a devotional. A young man with a beard got up to give it. His name was Joel Guillemette, from New York, and his fingers trembled a little on the pages.

He read a parable about a rich man who wanted to build some bigger barns so he could stockpile more grain and in that way be able to relax and enjoy himself and not have to worry so much. Jesus called him a fool. Then the preacher said that they and plenty of other people in town were like the rich man with the barns, except that with them it was snowmobiles, boats, and camps on South Twin and Ambejegus lakes.

"Watch out, and guard yourselves from all kinds of greed," he warned them from the book. "Because a man's true life is not made up of the things he owns, no matter how rich he may be."

When I looked around, the men were sitting and smiling politely up at the young man, as if he were talking about someone they knew slightly or had heard about.

I left the next day. The rain had taken the cold out of the air. Wiggie would have to be cutting up his deer.

I drove up the hill out of Millinocket, and at the place where Wiggie's old road joined the main road I looked between the roofs of the new houses, but the mountain was not there. Then I glanced the other way. The lights were flashing on the two great chimneys of the mill. White smoke billowed softly up into the dark rain clouds.

A few weeks later I got a telephone call from Fred Moore. He said that his brother's new wife, Yung, had arrived from Korea. Ho-Ja was happy because Yung was her best friend and now she was also her sister-in-law.

And that was not all. Ho-Ja had had her baby, a boy. He was born before the date the doctor had given him. He weighed six pounds, and they named him after his dad.

"Fred Moore the third," Fred said, and I could just see his smile. "Future wood poler." *– March 1981*

Wiggie's son Michael was killed in an accident in the paper room of the mill that dominates his resting place.

Glover, Vermont

IT MIGHT HAVE BEEN GLOVER. Before the Statue of Liberty came to rest in New York Harbor in 1886, there was a great debate about where this gift from France would best be located. Rivalries rose up among America's most prominent cities, all of whom made applications, causing *The New York Times* to cast its vote: "We have more than a million people in this city who are resolved that that great lighthouse statue shall be smashed into minute fragments before it shall be stuck up in Boston Harbor. If we are to lose the statue, it shall go to some worthier, more modest place ... Baltimore is a little late in her application ... The *Times* has always favored Glover, which has ... two churches, a liberal institute, and manufacturers of carriages, furniture, and boxes. Population: 1178."

Glover isn't as remote now, in 1986, as it was a hundred years ago, when traveling there from New York City could take six days or more. But it is still modest, and though the population is down to 846, perhaps there are still some reasons why it could be considered a fit home for the 305-foot mother of mercy.

Twenty miles south of the Canadian border, Glover's town lines are remarkably square, considering the ups and downs of its terrain. Most of the farms sit up on the hilltops, and the roads ride along the ridges of the hills, so that you are always looking back on another hill or another farm where the hayfields are like an open sea, so wide they just go on and on. Six miles square, Glover was named for its founder, General John Glover, who chartered the town in 1783, along with 62 other men and one woman. They were attracted to Glover's six lakes and many streams, which provided waterpower for industry, and its rich, black earth, good for farming. Perhaps they were also attracted to the

Extravagant dramatics of the Bread and Puppet Circus fill the town with activity one weekend each summer.

124

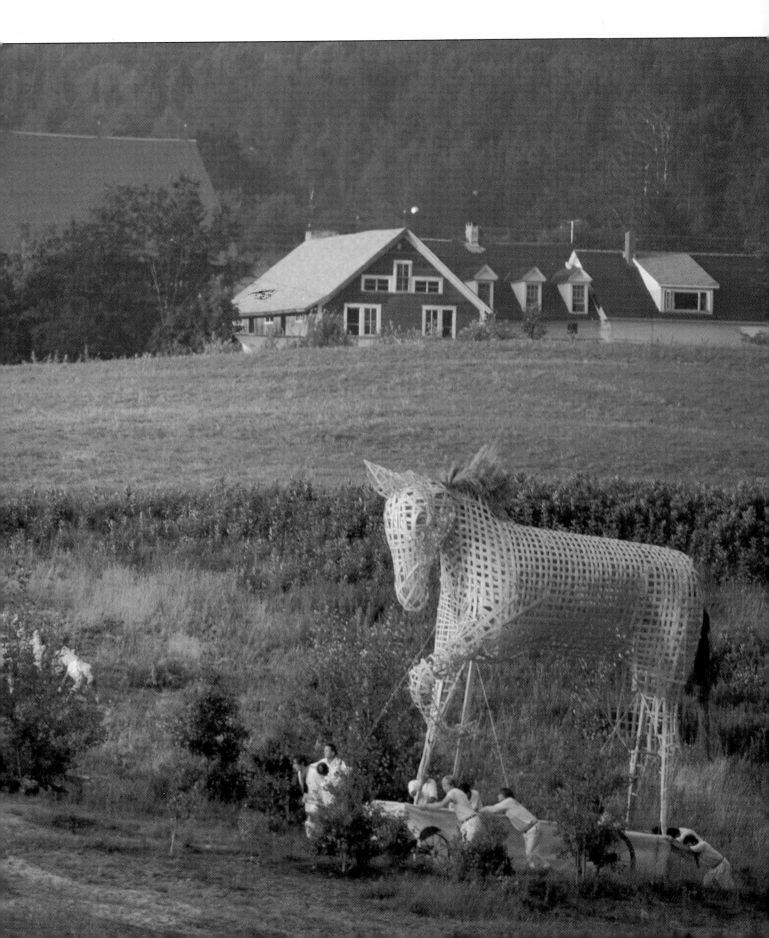

Text by Edie Clark • Photographs by Richard W. Brown

Lone Tree Hill, right in the center of this photo, was actually proposed and considered as a possible home for the Statue of Liberty *(left)*.

soft beauty of the round green hills that suggest peace.

From that modest beginning, Glover grew, and not much at that. There were no nearby cities to accommodate, no big industries that drew newcomers. So Glover just carried on, importing little and providing mostly for itself. In the Glover of a hundred years ago, it was far more possible to get what you needed in town than it is today. Between 1860 and 1880, Glover supported five blacksmiths, five boot- and shoemakers, a butcher, a carriage maker, a barber, a shingle mill, five coopers, a creamery, a dressmaker, three cabinetmakers, seven general stores, two gristmills, a gunsmith, two harness makers, a jeweler, ten doctors, four sawmills, three taverns, a tannery, a traveling troupe called Beedle & Prindle, and a taxidermist who doubled as the town's undertaker.

Glover, phenomenal in today's world of unfailing boom, has shrunk. There are no coopers or gristmills or blacksmiths left in Glover — in fact, there is no industry except a fence company. There are only two general stores now and a tiny, two-table diner called the Busy Bee. But there is still a traveling troupe in Glover, the Bread and Puppet Theater, and a taxidermist named Al Brooks who still holds forth,

from time to time, in his main street storefront.

"Glover is smaller now than it was when I was growing up," he said one morning last spring, a morning cool enough so that he had the potbellied stove fired up in his shop, where the

eyes of moose, black bears, foxes, pheasants, and fisher cats bear down on him from the walls and shelves all around. "The old blacksmith shop used to be here, and they used to have harness racing on the main street, which was still dirt then. They'd race

from here to the upper end of town. This would have been back in the thirties. They used to say that if you lived in Glover you'd have to own either a racehorse or a foxhound. Everybody used to fox hunt. A lot of people could work all week for ten or 12 dollars and then, if they went out on a Saturday and shot a fox, they could get 20 or 25 dollars. As good as working for two weeks straight. Course hunting wasn't as easy as it is now — there weren't any four-wheel drives or snowmobiles, no fancy guns or fancy scopes — you'd go out on your snowshoes with your dog. Everybody did it the hard way. Had to."

Al took over the business from his father Phil, and Al's son Mike works with him now, apprenticing into this increasingly rare trade. Al's family has lived in Glover for several generations,

and to hear him talk and to hear Mike talk that isn't likely to change. "Everybody knows everybody here. It's not like in a big city where you don't even know who lives in the next apartment. And you don't care who lives next to you. Down there everything is hustle-bustle and hurry up. You don't make as much money here, but I always figure you got two choices — you can go down to Massachusetts and make big money so you can spend that money to come back to Vermont to ski or hunt, or you can stay up in Vermont and make your $17,000 a year and have it right in your backyard."

He said he gets a kick out of thinking of the Statue of Liberty on top of Lone Tree Hill, a high round hill that's between Glover and West Glover. "I have a friend from New York — he comes up hunting every year. We told him that they were going to put the Statue of Liberty in Glover, and he says, 'No kiddin'! Nah!' He laughed, and then he said, 'Well, *we* got it!' He started thinking about it and he said, 'Yeah, I can

just see it up there on that hill,' and he started naming off people from town who'd be up there selling popcorn.

"Well, I've sat here trying to imagine that in my mind, and I just couldn't think what the area around it would be like. She'd be looking down on Lake Parker and on West Glover and maybe out over toward Canada. I mean, I've been down to New York and I've seen that statue a couple of different times, and a statue in a park is one thing, but a statue up on that hill in the middle of nowhere would be a little different. I was trying to imagine how they would have gotten it up there and what would have happened to those two farms up there. I mean, we could have all been millionaires just renting out the parking places."

Dean Bailey lives up across from Lone Tree Hill in a new split-level house he and his wife built when he returned to Glover after 22 years in the service. "Glover was my home when I left. I went into the Air Force when I was very young. I spent a lot of time in

Ada Urie (above) *works her garden in summer, selling plants and produce. Three generations of Rodgers dairy farmers* (right) *in front of their barn: John, Jim, and Craig, the youngest.*

the Far East — Japan, Korea, Guam, Vietnam — and England and the United States, too. I never even considered not coming back to Glover."

When he came back, the nation was gearing up for its bicentennial, and he and a group of other Glover residents began work on a town history. "We spent five or six years gathering information, looking back through old newspapers, cemeteries, and town records." It was then that Glover's bid for the Statue of Liberty came to light, and it was news to almost everyone in town. "I think there were just a few individuals in town who sent that letter in. I never really could prove anything about it with the exception of that paragraph in *The New York Times*. It's pretty obscure.

"I imagine that politics had a lot to

do with that. I mean, it was just a gift, a statue, and they had to decide where to put it. I don't think when they set her up they thought it would be such a big deal as it is today. But even so, in Glover? We're unheard of all over. That statue looks pretty good to me down there, right where it is."

Dean looks directly out at Lone Tree Hill, through his south window. In fact, almost every wall in his house has picture windows. Through one he looks down into the village of West Glover and through another he says that on a clear day he can see the tram running back and forth on Jay Peak, which is up on the Canadian border. And, as if he cannot bear a wall without a view, on the wall between the living room and the dining room he has a painting of West Glover village, quite like the real view out his west window.

"Years ago, a view didn't mean anything — they didn't build on a hill, they built where they'd be protected from the wind. They didn't care about what they were looking at. But I love this. I can sit and eat breakfast and look out and see deer feeding and a lot of other animals coming and going. I mean, to me, that's pretty nice."

Like many others in Glover, Dean Bailey likes the town the way it is. "I like the independence. I can walk just about anywhere and I'm not trespassing. We lived outside of Burlington in Essex Junction for five years and I saw how it changed when IBM moved in. It made a tremendous change to that area. Glover hasn't seen changes like that. You'll see some new homes scattered here and there, but that's about the only change that I know of."

In the sixties and seventies, though, there were changes in Glover, as there were in so many Vermont towns that suddenly became havens for young people who sought a simpler life. Cabins sprang up on land where no one thought anyone would or should build, and run-down farmhouses became home to groups of long-haired, nature-loving youths. In 1974 Peter and Elka Schumann chose Glover as the home for their Bread and Puppet Theater, a repertory company already well known for their giant outdoor puppet shows and parades, which carried messages against war and nuclear power and pro-

Town historians, among them, Dean Bailey, above, discovered Glover's bid to be the home of Miss Liberty.

moted art as sustenance. When Dean came back from the service, the Bread and Puppet had only just moved to Glover. "When I came back, they were just getting started and there were communes — a lot of young people had come to Glover then, more or less to live off the land. But that's all gone now. I mean, some of them who came are still here, but they've got electricity and they're getting up and going out to work just like the rest of us. They're part of the community. This living off the land business is over."

The Schumanns' Bread and Puppet Theater is still there, however, and Our Domestic Resurrection Circus, the show that they have put on in Glover every summer for the past 12 years, is still bringing 15,000 to 20,000 people to Glover from all over the world. Many people in Glover have come to appreciate the circus for the art that it represents, and in fact many Gloverites act as extras at the circus.

"You can see them practicing up in their field a long time before they put on the show," Dean Bailey said. "That's a different form of the arts. I don't care for the political portions of it, but the talent is just unbelievable. The Fourth of July used to be a big deal here in town, but it got to be too much

so we cut it out. But now the Bread and Puppet Circus is the big weekend in town. That's about all we need."

The Bread and Puppet Theater was founded 20 years ago in New York's Lower East Side by German-born sculptor Peter Schumann. At first he worked out of a loft, and annual productions of the Christmas and Easter stories were an important part of the repertory, as were demonstrations against the war in Vietnam, using over-lifesized puppets and masked performers in parades and street shows. In 1970 he moved the Theater to Vermont and then to Glover when he and his wife Elka bought the old Dopp farm. In the barn they made a museum to house all the hundreds of masks and puppets, using the horse stalls to stage the smaller puppets and the haymow for the towering 16- and 18-foot masks. The museum is free and open year round.

Bread and Puppet has come to represent a lot to Glover, and one of the most important things is perhaps this worldliness that nothing else, other than perhaps the Statue of Liberty, could have brought them. Chris Braithwaite is the publisher of *The Chronicle,* a newspaper with a circulation of 6,500 that serves Glover and the other 18 towns and villages of Orleans County. Chris lives in West Glover and has taken part in many of the Bread and Puppet productions, not only in Glover, but also traveling with them to New York City and to London. He admires Glover's tolerance. "One of the nicest things about Glover is the easy ability to get along between the people who've been there for five generations and those who arrived in the sixties and seventies." He finds this true also of Bread and Puppet. "It's kind of wonderful. They'll take the puppets that they march through the streets of New York and bring them up here and march them in a local parade. They don't play down to a local audience. In fact, lots of their productions that have played all over the world premiered in Vermont. *Diagonal Man* is one of their best known — it played in Poland, France, Germany, Austria — but it premiered right here."

Elka Schumann is originally from Connecticut, and she does not always go on tour with her husband and the

Horses are still popular, as Ken and Sue Swift (above) *show, but when Laban Darling* (left) *was blacksmith there was harness racing on Main St.*

touring company, preferring instead to stay at home in Glover much of the year. She feels that when a particular show plays first in Glover (which is not uncommon, since that is where they put many of the productions together), it is sometimes like playing first for the family. "It's like family because many of our neighbors take part in it. Well, when I say neighbors, you have to un-derstand there aren't many people around here, so neighbors can be as far as 20 miles away." Their remote loca-tion suits them still. In Glover they will stay. "It is very small, very friendly, very rural. I don't know if there is anything like it. Well, I was in Scotland once and it looked like Vermont, yes, Vermont without trees."

Many of Glover's early settlers in fact came there from Scotland. The oldest section of town is known as An-dersonville, settled by Scots named An-derson who intermarried there with other Scots — Patersons and Youngs and Uries. Ada Drew married Will Urie and the two of them were well known in Glover, Will for his stern re-fusal to farm with a tractor, keeping his horses instead, and Ada for the fresh vegetables and the breads and dough-nuts and pies that she still sells to the summer people who come to cabins on Lake Parker and Shadow Lake. People speak fondly of driving by the Uries' farm to see Will and Ada in their field scything the hay. Will died a few years ago, but Ada still lives at Sunnyside, which they bought during the Depres-sion and gradually fixed up. Her gar-dens are the envy of many. "I've been here all my life," she said, sitting in the kitchen of her daughter Mary's house, "85 years. And I've never once wanted to be anyplace but here. I know every-one and everyone knows me. This is home."

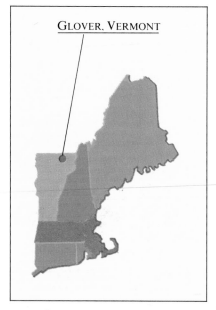

GLOVER, VERMONT

Ada is a pretty lady with fine-boned hands that speak for her when she can't think of a word. She makes her gray hair into braids and ties them up over her head in a half-circle, as she always has. She was born in a lumber camp her father ran on Black Hill in Glover, and her life has been all Glover, though every summer she and Will would take off to climb another of Vermont's mountains. "Always for our anniversary Will and I went on a trip in the car with our camping equipment. We have climbed a lot of the mountains here in Vermont. I love mountains. We have to like them around here! But they're cutting more and more of the forests. I hope they don't cut them too much, because Vermont wouldn't be Vermont without our hills and our trees."

She says she has not seen many changes in Glover, only in the roads, which, even though most of the 60-some-odd miles of roads in Glover are still unpaved and tended only by a two-man crew, she thinks are a lot better. "I don't remember when we did get scraped roads — can you remember, Mary?" she asked, turning to her daughter, who was bent over the kitchen counter, rolling out cookie dough. "Yes, '38 or '39. We used to keep the car down at the main road and drive the team down to it. I still remember the time when we went to town to do the shopping and started home. We got just beyond Shadow Lake and the car

went right up to the running board. We had a load of groceries and a great big Easter lily in the back for one of the neighbors. We would jack one wheel up and by the time we'd get that jacked up and went around, the other one was down. Oh, that mud — it was *just* bearable! When we didn't come back, my husband and my daughter figured we were stuck, and they came down with the horses and hitched the work har-

ness to the car and we got out that way. In those days, if you had a wagon, you were all right, but not with a car. The roads now are some different from what they used to be."

And Ada Urie laments the prevalence of regional schools. Glover's high-school students are bused to a regional school in Orleans. "There aren't any rural schools anymore. When I was growing up there was a school in every

district, and some districts wouldn't have more than four or five students. They measured the distance between each district so that the kids could walk to school. I don't think there were more than six in my school. Let's see, there was Leslie and Floyd and William and Melvin and myself, and I don't remember if there were two Cook girls or just one. The school year was different then — there was no school in February be-cause of the snow and no school in March because of the mud. Then we'd be in school till the last of June. We always had a picnic at the end down at Shadow Lake."

She knows about the Bread and Pup-pet Theater but she's never seen their show because she doesn't drive a car. But of them she said, "They've certain-ly put Glover on the map. They say that people come from far away to go to it. They hold it outside, in a field that's like a theater. You know, the hills slide right down and people can sit on the grass and look down on it. I guess it really is very nice."

But the curious fact that it might have been Glover instead of New York City was news to her. "Oh?" she said. Her bright eyes lit up and she laughed so that she rocked a little in her chair. "My!"

– July 1986

133

Richmond, Maine

I T BEGAN WITH A DREAM — RO-
mantic, yet also practical, and
maybe just a little opportunis-
tic. Vladimir Kuhn von Poushental, born a baron in the
Russian Empire of the Czar, an officer
in the Russian Air Force, later exiled as
an active anti-Communist during
World War II, came to the Kennebec
Valley in Maine in 1952 and saw his
future. The land had been ravaged by
the fierce fires of the summer of 1947.
Farms were either abandoned or selling
for $2,000 or less. He was struck by the
landscape, scarred as it was. The rolling
hills, the tree-lined river, the forests
filled with mushrooms, reminded him
of the Russian countryside. He knew
that hundreds of fellow Russians and
people from neighboring Slavic coun-
tries had sought exile in America, as he
had done, after fighting in vain against
the Russian Revolution. A business-
man who had already made a tidy fortune, Poushental promptly began
buying homesteads in the valley, con-
centrating his attention on the small riverfront town of Richmond. Then he

*Exiled White Russians brought their
enduring faith with them to Richmond.*

by Mel Allen • Photographs by Carole Allen

Father German Ciuba, pastor of St. Alexander-Nevsky Russian Orthodox Church Abroad, beside the Kennebec.

Mrs. Tatiana Zilin and her son Sasha. A noted opera singer in her homeland, Mrs. Zilin was fortunate to find that her talents were in demand in her adopted country.

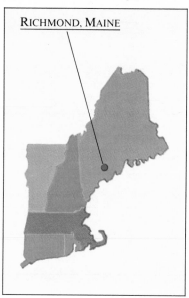

RICHMOND, MAINE

The Balalaika Orchestra plays traditional Slavic and East European music around the area.

began advertising throughout North America in the Russian newspapers.

One woman remembers the advertisements. "Oh, he said, 'Come to Maine. Hunting, fishing, cheap land. And we would be together, speaking our own language, in a good climate.'"

So they came. Nearly all were White Russians, who at times during the Russian Civil War had succeeded in inflicting heavy losses on the Red Army; but by 1920 their forces had been crushed, and they scattered. One woman murmured to me, "I have seen the world in the hardest way."

Many had been born to a now vanished aristocracy, studying at the finest schools in Europe, and were fluent in many languages, English rarely being one of them: Ivan Tolstoy, grandson of the revered Russian novelist, who would direct the choir in the St. Alexander-Nevsky Russian Orthodox Church; Tatiana Zilin, an opera singer who speaks only Russian with her American-born son; Eugene Sherbakoff, an actor from Odessa who, prior to coming to Maine, began a revival of the Russian theater in New York; his wife, Alexandra, a ballerina and concert singer in her youth who found work in a Richmond shoe factory. Arriving too were former rural Russians who had worked their farms, who were sturdy, filled with stamina, eager to build homes and raise chickens. Within a few years, more than a hundred Russians had arrived in the Kennebec Valley, and two Russian Orthodox churches and one Ukrainian church had sprung up in the quiet Maine village. By the mid-1960s perhaps 500

Russians and Slavs had completed what one called "the gentle invasion." Television, newspapers, and magazines invaded as well, fascinated with what had suddenly become the largest Russian community in rural America.

There were charming, sometimes touching stories of assimilation — a Russian going into a general store followed by his four goats; a burly Russian farmer hoisting a 100-pound sack of grain on his shoulders and walking with it the five miles to his home. A Maine man who moved into an old house in Richmond on a street with Russian neighbors wrote: ". . . Petrya has a daughter in Kiev whom he has not seen in many years. He has her picture on a bureau with her letters piled up before it like offerings before an icon. . . . One of the other times I was at the house, Petrya pointed to his shortwave radio and said, 'Kiev, Moscow, Leningrad.' I murmured 'St. Petersburg,' and he hugged me and said 'Da, Da, St. Petersburg!' " Sometimes tourists would come during the colorful Easter service (*Yankee,* April 1961), and for a time you could not think of Richmond without thinking of Russians. Today there are perhaps 100 Russians in Richmond, 100 more in nearby towns. The center of their life remains their church, and the touchstone of its influence remains the Russian Easter, the holiday of hope.

I first saw Richmond on a blustery spring morning ten years ago. We had nearly driven past the small town park by the river when we saw three men and three women walking toward us. They wore long black coats, the men in

The St. Alexander-Nevsky Russian Orthodox Church, named for a general, is one of two in town.

fur hats, the women wrapped in scarves; I had not seen their like before in Maine. We parked the car and walked. The streets in Richmond rise sharply from the river, but I don't think we noticed. We were staring at the onion-shaped dome and the three-armed gold cross on top of the Russian church.

We turned a corner and found a res-taurant that served borsch, beef Stroga-noff, and pirozhki. On the main street was a small cobbler shop where a Rus-sian bootmaker made leather riding boots, and on the outskirts of the town we wandered through a cemetery where, clustered in the southwest cor-ner, there were Byzantine crosses and the stones of the Russian dead, their graves lined with fresh flowers.

Unlike the Finns and Swedes who came to Maine during earlier genera-tions, most of the Russians were past middle age; there were few baptisms, and many funerals — a solemn service during which the mourners file by the body in the center of the church to give a last kiss. A few years ago the restau-rant closed and the bootmaker retired. The parties of the Slavophile Society grew more subdued, and, when his wife died, Ivan Tolstoy moved to Jordan-ville, New York, which had overtaken Richmond as the largest Russian rural community.

It was crowded in the church that night, the holiday bringing families to-gether like Christmas. We stood bathed in candlelight, waiting for the service to begin at 11:30. This was Father Ger-man Ciuba's first Easter with his parish in St. Alexander-Nevsky Church. He is youthful enough at 27 to be the grand-son of most of his parishioners, yet they kissed his hand in reverence, calling him Batiushka (Little Father). Just be-fore midnight we filed outside, walking solemnly around the small church. The people carried candles, banners, and food to be blessed; the air was sweet with incense. It was midnight when Fa-ther German halted on the steps and said, "Khristos Voskresse." ("Christ is risen.") It was cold outside and the peo-ple pressed close together as they chanted, "Voistinu, Voskresse." ("In truth, He is risen.") They turned then and embraced.

The service wound into the early morning; there were no pews, and peo-ple stood unless fatigue made them rest on a few benches tucked into the cor-ners. Filled with mystery and symbol-ism, the night fascinated me; I lingered in the empty church pondering a ques-tion I dared to ask as we stood outside. It was 4 A.M. and the Russians were going home to feast.

"What will happen to the church," I asked an elderly woman, "when there are only a few of you left?" There was no mourning in her voice when she said, "Someday there will be nobody, and only at Easter when the young peo-ple return will there be a service."

Maybe in ten years, give or take a few, Richmond will no longer boast of a Russian community; there will still be Russians and Slavs, but again they will be scattered. But they hadn't come for riches, simply for a home, and that they will keep until there is no one left to give the last kiss.

– April 1980

Mr. Urkanov reads a Russian paper in the library of the St. Alexander-Nevsky Foundation.

Freedom, New Hampshire

by Edie Clark • Photographs by Dean Abramson

DOWN IN THE TOWN THE streets are still narrow and the white clapboard houses sit close to the granite curbs. White picket fences and lilac hedges draw lines between neighbors. The village store is still there, but all that's left of the tanneries and mills are stone foundations and cellar holes near the brook, trees growing from their centers.

The pamphlet town history put out 26 years ago has a title like a statement of victory: "125 Years of Freedom." Freedom can't help its double entendre — the name came after an all-but-forgotten squabble that took place when the town broke away from Effingham in 1832.

Freedom is 27 square miles, shaped like a pennant, with a terrain that includes seven lakes and ponds, a river and countless streams, and two mountains. The territory is so rough that the town once supported eight different schools, laid out so the children in each district could walk to school. Along the brook that races through town there were four tanneries, a sawmill, a grist mill, and a mill that made bobbins, rakes, and chairs. There was a machine shop, a tinsmith shop, a harness shop, and a tar factory. During the 1800s there was a bank, the Ossipee Valley Ten Cent Bank, in Freedom. Throughout the past 151 years, Freedom has maintained a population that's never reached a thousand, and today, at 767, it's not too far from what it was at the turn of the century. In the summer, though, it's much more, twice that, maybe more.

For early Old Home Week, buckboard carried Freedomites to a ballgame.

With its lakes and trout ponds, and hills that offer wide views of distant blue hills, Freedom has long attracted summer visitors, summer boarders, summer homeowners. It's been the summer population that's sustained Freedom since the mills shut down and the bank left town. That little town history talks about the houses in town more than the founding families. It notes who built them and recounts the succession of owners since. Most of the first families are gone, but the houses endure, perhaps in better repair today than they ever were. The summer people bought them, the old farms and the houses in the village — fixing them up, fussing over them, preserving them like a historic district before there ever was such a thing.

Nelson Works, Peter Case, and George Davidson are three summer people who came to stay. Their love for Freedom is in some ways stronger than that of native sons, and they give back to the town in the very best sense.

Nelson Works, along with others, runs the Freedom Museum. In fact, he's the founder, the curator, and the chief benefactor of the three-story barn near the center of town. Nelson Works grew up in Freedom, summers, and says he's old enough to remember what life in Freedom was like before the hard roads came. Though his career in world banking took him to live in places as far away as Australia, he thinks of Freedom as his hometown, the only continuous home he's ever known. Six years ago, he gratefully retired to Freedom year-round, which gave him more time to devote to the museum. A stern, crusty fellow, Nelson Works has a soft center when it comes to Freedom. Over the years he's put many thousands of dollars into this museum, through which he leads visitors as if it were his home, demonstrating how to use an early eggbeater and cutting a quick pattern with the treadle jigsaw. The museum is attached to what was Margie's Lunch back in the fifties; alongside the knowledgeably labeled tools and carriages and old stoves is the sign she hung from the porch, and in the glass case next to a collection of early toys and tobacco tins is a framed snapshot of Margie herself. There is a lot in the museum, though, that's not from Freedom, items that came from Texas and Bali, all of which somehow say as much about Freedom as the Margie's Lunch sign.

Across the street from the museum, Peter Case lives in the old Amos Towle house. Peter Case is what Nelson Works would call an "immigrant" — he came to Freedom four years ago, taking refuge from a high-pressure

Tradition began in 1898 and continues strong today. About half the townspeople dress up and march in the colorful Old Home Week Parade.

It is Freedom's lakes and ponds that cause the town's population to at least double every summer.

A competitive firemen's muster (above) is also part of Old Home Week. There's always room for another vehicle, no matter the size, in the parade (left), since the whole affair usually takes only ten minutes to go through town.

broadcasting job in New York City. He brought with him his children, his dark good looks, and a deep reserve of enthusiasm. He went into business for himself, making mustard there in Amos's old kitchen, and now is the chairman of Old Home Week, pouring endless energy into designing T-shirts, wooing the U.S. Army Band to the parade, and trying to convince President Reagan to attend these festivities that bring thousands of Freedom-lovers back to town. "Nobody's *from* Freedom," Peter Case points out, and then ticks off a list of his neighbors. "They came from New Jersey, and the people next door to them came up from Connecticut two years ago. Freedom is what you think of when you think of hometown. It's almost corny. Flags go-

FREEDOM, NEW HAMPSHIRE

The Freedom Cornet Band (top), *founded in 1886, performed for over 20 years and surely played at early Old Home gatherings. Peter Case waits with friends* (above) *for the start of the parade. Ralph and Madeline Eldridge* (right) *relax on their porch on Village Road.*

ing up the flagpoles *every day.* Picket fences and white clapboards. Screened front porches and flowers in the front. The town where I grew up in Connecticut was like this — once."

Around the corner is the First Christian Church of Freedom, of which George Davidson has been minister for the past 30 years. Growing up in suburban Boston, George Davidson went to summer camp in Freedom. The beauty there made such an impression on him that, while he was stationed in the Pacific during World War II, he dreamed of Freedom and tried to imagine how he could one day make it his home. After the war George Davidson came back to Freedom as a lay minister to cover the Easter service. He's been there ever since. A lean stalk of a man, George now lives with his family in a

144

house at the edge of a 15-acre trout pond, near where he went to camp back in the twenties. "I feel that the Good Lord had something to do with that," is the conclusion he draws. Many in town refer to him as the backbone of Freedom. The Reverend Davidson admits that he occasionally can't resist taking liberties with the word *freedom* in his sermons. "Freedom of choice — I use that one a lot. But you don't want to overdo it."

It's hard not to. Nelson Works knew Freedom as the town before he knew it as a concept. "When I was a little boy, and they used to say 'let freedom ring,' I thought they meant the hills and rocks and brooks all around here. It took me a long time to figure out they weren't talking about Freedom."

– July 1983

Marblehead, Massachusetts

by Edie Clark • Photographs by Ulrike Welsch

OOK DOWN EISENHOWER Road or Johns Drive and the comfortable split-levels and capes set on small lots make Marblehead look like any other suburban community within easy commuting distance of a major city. But Marblehead's history goes back a lot further than the MBTA or Route 128, and patriotism underlies this town like a deep underground reservoir that cannot be depleted.

Marblehead is a 2,816-acre cape shaped like a monkey wrench with a harbor in its grip. If you try to square it off, it has seven sides, six of which meet the water either as riverfront, oceanfront, harborfront, or beachfront. The harbor is twice as long as it is wide and is filled to capacity with 2,300 moorings — a few for lobster boats, but many for exquisite racing yachts. The town is known as the yachting capital of the world, and in keeping with that it has six yacht clubs, one of them the oldest in New England and another one just for children.

Though the population surpasses 20,000, there is much in Marblehead that becomes a small town. Narrow streets and brick walkways pass at eye level to the windows of the houses that follow the crooked lines of the streets. There is no industry, except for what the yachting and tourism bring in. There are no fast-food restaurants or strips of gas stations and convenience malls. In fact, though thousands of tourists pass through town every year, there are no motels and only a few places for visitors to stay: they can rent a room in a big old yellow house with fans in the windows for hot nights, flowered wallpaper, and wide oak doors with glass doorknobs.

The town has served as a backdrop for movies shot during the 1920s, as well as for some 1970s pictures, and no doubt it looked much the same then as it does now. Eugene O'Neill lived there and so did George Bernard Shaw.

Marblehead does not cordon off its history, putting it all in a museum, but instead lives inside its tradition, a practice which, for a town just 16 miles outside Boston, allows for some complications. In the historic district, which is much of the downtown area, there is row upon row of 200-year-old houses with gambrel roofs and widow's walks and scuttles that open up out of the roof like a hatch on a ship. There are alleyways, narrow as young girls, and tiny yards with lettuce growing in window boxes and roses blooming high up on trellises. There is a legend on every corner, and, like stately dowagers, the houses are protected by their legacies and lineages. Many have wooden plaques near the front door that tell who the original owner was and what he did for a living. In a sense, these houses cannot be owned, only looked after: owners cannot modernize the houses outside of the rigid historic code and must attend a hearing even for permission to change a doorway.

Marblehead is big enough to consider itself a city, but it prefers to maintain its status as a town. Like other small New England communities, Marblehead has a town government made up of a board of selectmen and a town clerk, and they still use the annual town meeting forum to make major town decisions. Motions have been made to install computers in the town hall, but they have been defeated, and votes are still cast on paper ballots and counted by hand.

In addition, there is the problem faced by all cities: what to do with all the cars. There's a joke that occasional-

Rooftops in the historic district suggest the pattern of the crooked streets.

ly makes the rounds on the North Shore: a person convicted of traffic violations could be sentenced to 99 years in downtown Marblehead. To approach downtown Marblehead is to disappear into a thicket of one-way streets and loops and dead ends, and there is a risk that if you don't know your way around you might leave without ever having seen the harbor. A car in Marblehead is often a liability, and seeing the town by foot is always the

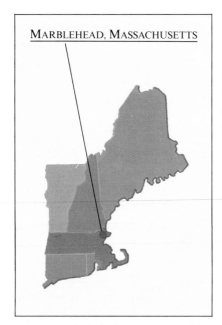

MARBLEHEAD, MASSACHUSETTS

Hurricane Gloria deposited the beautiful *Ansa*, beyond repair, on the rocks of Crowninshield Island.

recommendation. Problems of parking and traffic flow are perennial ones, often discussed at town meetings. There are apparently few solutions: the winding streets are part of the heritage, and in Marblehead considerations of tradition and history far outweigh conveniences sought by the modern world.

With streets and coves and beaches named after local patriotic heroes — Devereaux, Abbot, Glover, Gerry — pride runs high in Marblehead. One of the town's most prized possessions is the painting known as "The Spirit of '76," the often-reproduced painting of the fife-and-drum corps marching determinedly under a stormy sky. The painting is huge, the figures larger than life, and it hangs in the Selectmen's Room in the town hall, which is as much a museum as it is a government center. For the past 24 years Elizabeth McKinnon has served as secretary for the selectmen. Her desk sits facing the painting, past which some 60,000 visitors file every year. Some days Mrs. McKinnon has a hard time getting her work done in between answering the questions of inquisitive tourists. In this aspect, she is patient and tireless but, when asked if perhaps the painting ought to be moved so that she could get her work done more easily, she said, "Well, maybe they could build a partition around me, or move me. But they would *never* move the painting."

– September 1982

Strafford, Vermont

by Edie Clark • Photographs by Richard W. Brown

Beautiful hillside farmsteads
belie the miles of mining shafts
under Strafford's rolling hills.

B
Y MAP, STRAFFORD IS AS square-edged as a blanket, but by car, the roads that pass by the pastures and fields of this eastern Vermont town are more like a carnival ride. Everything is uphill or downhill; nothing is across. And what is more striking is the openness, how you can see so far into the next valley. And into the next.

Strafford is really two towns — Strafford, known as the upper village, and South Strafford, the lower village. Strafford is where the town house is, which sits up on a hill and looks down on the common and the white clapboard, tin-roofed houses that ring it. South Strafford is where the store is and where the school is, which also sits up on a hill and looks down at the white clapboard, tin-roofed houses that line the road that leads to the old copper mine. But, though both towns have their own town centers, their own post offices, and their own churches, ask just about anyone in either place and they'll say without hesitation that it's all one town.

Joseph Maclay moved to South Strafford in 1945 because of the copper mine. It was during the war, the need for copper was great, and the Elizabeth Mine was at that time an important source of copper. "We were in a hurry to buy a house, my wife and I. Jessie wanted a place where she could walk to the store, something near town. When

STRAFFORD, VERMONT

we heard about this house, even though it was nighttime, we went over and the man showed us through with a kerosene lantern. It looked all right to us. It was to be cash, so we took a suitcase full of money down to the town clerk's office where we made the deal. But then, when the light dawned and I saw the rotted sills and floorboards — oh! — I could have slit my wrists!"

The copper mine closed down in 1958, sending many of the more than 240 miners to work in other copper mines in North Carolina and Canada. Originally from Scotland, Joe could also have gone elsewhere to work after the mine closed, but Jessie, a native Vermonter, wouldn't budge from South Strafford, and he softened on the idea of leaving since the round, smooth hills around the town reminded him so much of his homeland.

"We had people come and people go, but Jessie and I really became part of the local community," he says, his voice still thick with a Scottish brogue. "A lot of the miners did leave, though. They had to. There was no work for them here."

In those days nearly everyone in Strafford had something to do with the mine. Many of the houses and some of the farms in town were "company houses" — houses owned by the mine, where the miners lived as part of their pay. The shafts of the mine bored down under the town for two miles, running deceptively beneath the hayfields. And every day the town trembled and the thunder of the dynamite blasts could be heard underneath the earth, extending the mine shaft just that much farther, and bringing up 800 tons of ore daily. On Fridays the men would crowd into Varney's Store and line up to cash their checks, for there was no bank closer than Hanover, New Hampshire.

Even the farmers were miners, sandwiching their chores in between their shifts at the mine. The mine brought newcomers into town and gave the town a sense of worldliness not shared by other Vermont towns. "When the mine closed down, everyone thought that the town would fold completely," Rosa Tyson says. "But of course it didn't. This is beautiful country. We began to get summer people. There's really nothing to do here — no golf course or lake or anything like that. But it's so

The Strafford of today is home to pleasure horses as well as dairy cattle.

beautiful. People just come."

Today Strafford is a town of newcomers who have stayed. There probably isn't a more solid old-timer in town than Rosa Tyson, but the Tysons came first as summer people, way back in the early 19th century, when the trip from Baltimore took them six days by boat and by stage.

It was Rosa Tyson's great-grandfa-

ther, Isaac Tyson, who first became interested in Strafford's copper. Local people had known there was copper there since 1793, but Isaac Tyson was the first to make a business out of it. Although the business went out of the Tysons' hands in the early part of this century, the family stayed, and Rosa, who was born in 1900 on the same day her grandfather died, says that, for her, it was always Strafford. The Elizabeth Mine was named after her grandmother, Elizabeth Tyson, and Buena Vista,

the house where Rosa was born and where she still lives, is on Mine Road, about half a mile from the entrance. "The mine," she says, "was home." Rosa remembers when there were mules working down in the mine, bringing up cartloads of ore. And she remembers when the ore was taken by ox cart to Pompanoosuc, where it was loaded on trains and taken all the way to Long Island. And she remembers going down into the mine when she was a little girl: "It was dark and scary!" she

exclaims, her sharp eyes lighting up mischievously.

"I went to school in Boston for a while and, after that, I taught in Baltimore, but my mother and father weren't well, so I came home and I've been here ever since." After the Tysons sold the mine, they started a girls' camp there at the house and down by the river. "We called it Kenjocketee," Rosa explains. "That means 'beyond the multitude,' which of course it always was and it still is."

"I WAS BLOWN UP ONE NIGHT WAY down in the shaft," Joe Maclay recalls. "A blast that should have gone off one, two, three, four, went off all together. I was down on the 575 level (575 feet) and it blew out the lights and I landed down in the water. My hat got blown off and with it went my light. There were tracks up through the shaft for the rail cars to haul the ore, and I crawled up on my hands and knees in the dark, all the way, holding onto the rail. I was lucky. I just got a few scratches."

Like an abandoned village, the mine is still there. It is posted, no trespassing, but Joe Maclay can go there and pry up bits of memories like those. Though there are others left in the area who worked at the mine — Gordon Tracy, Harlow Lent, Jack Josler — there are only a few who can still speak the language of the mines — talk about stopes and adits, drifts and raises, benches and brows. When the mine closed, they left a desert of tailings (the waste product of the milling process) that stretches out among the softness of the blue-green hills like a shimmering orange mirage. And all around it the water runs red, and there are little copper-colored rivulets that streak the roads. Above it the hills are cut away, their insides exposed,

Rosa Tyson (left) *still lives in the house built by her great-grandfather Isaac Tyson* (below). *In the forties, men came from all over the world to work the copper mines* (bottom), *until they were all closed in 1958. They remain so today* (far left).

spilling out and down the cliffs, merging with the mountains of waste ore left behind like a new geology. The mill and the workshops and the changehouse, where the men would shower and change after coming up out of the mine, are still there, doors hanging open, poplars growing up through the porch floors, up through the iron buckets. The valley is completely filled with tailings — most of it made during

World War II. Joe points out the depth of the pile, which rises up out of the valley so completely that it nearly meets the height of the neighboring hills. "We are the ones who built it up. It was way, way down when the mine started up again in 1942. In some places they moved the tailings and used it for fill or something else. But nothing's ever been done here.

"Come, there is more that I want you to see," he says. Joe is 82 but does not hesitate. We climb up the steep, high pile of waste rock, letting slabs, hot from the sun, tumble down the sheer, sheer slope. Crows as big as eagles perch on top of the cliffs and yack and scold. The view from on top, next to the open cut — a deep gouge in the earth where miners in the very early days crouched in crawl spaces to coax the ore out of the vein with hand picks — is panoramic, spectacular. Hills riffle off, step after step, like swells on the open sea. "It's a shame," he says, "tragic!" He is quiet, then: "I agree we've ruined a beautiful valley, but what are you going to do for strategic metals? They needed the stuff!"

But the mine is off by itself in a little corner in the southern part of town, and if you were just passing through, you wouldn't know it was there. Which maybe is more the point than the pile of tailings left behind. Years back you couldn't have passed through the town without knowing the mine was there.

There isn't anything that has a hold on Strafford now the way the mine once did — except maybe its enduring beauty. Early this past summer a San Francisco advertising agency picked Strafford to be used as a backdrop for a salad-dressing commercial. "We were looking for a beautiful town in a valley with a high steeple," film producer Robert Casey says. "We wanted an attitude — something that would read New England, Small Town, U.S.A. We looked at about 40 towns. For what we had to do, there wasn't a lot of choice — Strafford was always high on the list. Their town house is the most dramatic one I've ever seen. I mean, it just stands there like a monolith." They came, about a 45-member crew in vans, and

Joe Maclay, drawn to the soft hills, stayed when other miners moved on.

hired some 40 local people as extras. They staged a potluck supper at the town house, and they painted Russell Farley's barn with giant green letters — HIDDEN VALLEY RANCH — and filmed it from a helicopter.

Kathy Wert, who serves as Strafford's town clerk, helped make arrangements for the commercial, and she and her husband and two small children acted as extras at the mock supper. The Werts have lived in Strafford for seven years. Like Joe Maclay, Kathy came here and stayed here because it reminds her of her home. "I grew up in northern Connecticut, Litchfield County, which has been called 'a little corner of Vermont.' That's true. This is very much like where I grew up.

"There was some tension last year when Newmont Mining Company came around this area, checking out mining rights. There was a helicopter flying around for weeks. Everyone was aware of it, but no one knew what was going on. There were all kinds of rumors. Some people thought they wanted to reopen the mine. Some people thought they were looking for gold. I don't think, though, that anything will come of it all.

"A lot of people in town are active — active in the antinuclear movement and the peace movement. We're kind of known for that now. It's special, and people know that; they are willing to

make the extra commute to live here and work in Hanover. It wasn't always like this — even in the last ten years there's been a big change. Three out of five of our justices of the peace are Democrats. It used to be a very Republican town.

"The big issue this year was the school. There was a vote to raise a $1-million bond to build a new school, and it was very divisive. Not just locals versus newcomers, but money versus no money, kids versus no kids. It was a big turmoil, but I think it will pass. There's a strong sense of community here. People really care about each other. Like the commercial. They looked at many towns from the air and from every angle, and they could see that this was really a community."

The changes for this town of 735 are many and they are few, and almost always they have come from the outside. But in the scheme of the world, the changes are small. Last year in Strafford, six people died and six babies were born.

Jessie Maclay passed away three years ago, but Joe still lives in the house he bought with a suitcase full of cash from a man who showed it to him on a moonless night by the light of a kerosene lantern. He's long since fixed up the sills and the floors, and he and Jessie raised five children there — one of his sons lives five houses down in one of the old company houses. Joe's house is next to the cemetery, where he and Jessie have a plot so close that the picket fence from his yard runs along behind the stone and some of the limbs from his apple tree give it shade. Some of the changes in town bother him — too many bleeding hearts, he says, and it will never again be the way it was when the mine was running. And so Joe talks about moving, maybe getting an apartment somewhere closer to White River Junction where he works. Joe Maclay does as he pleases — he got his college degree when he was 78, and is working toward his master's — but would he really move away from Strafford? "It's been a pretty nice life," he says, "all things considered."

– October 1985

158

Harlow Lent, philosopher and editor of *Muckraker Sweet,* once worked at the mine.

Greenville, Maine

by Mel Allen • Photographs by Carole Allen

Moosehead Lake is the gateway to some ten
million acres of Maine forest, and nearly all
of its 350-mile shoreline remains undeveloped.

FROM THE BEGINNING, people came to Greenville hunting for something. The Abnakis were first, seeking flint for arrowheads on Kineo Mountain. White men came for the white pine that became spars and masts on coastal schooners and for the spruce that became pulp. Trains from Boston brought sportsmen for Moosehead Lake's fabled fishing or for caribou hunting, when great herds a mile long still roamed, and one could hear the sound of horns cracking together long before sighting the caribou. Thoreau came, and Teddy Roosevelt, and Ulysses S. Grant. Prizefighters came to be toughened in the logging camps, and as many as 27 steamboats plied the lake carrying passengers and freight.

But it was a town and a way of life vulnerable to the 20th century. The caribou migrated to Canada; so did the wolves. Crosscut saws replaced axes, chain saws replaced crosscuts, and eventually machinery replaced logging camps. Roads replaced legendary river drives. Fishing declined, and Moosehead depended on hatcheries for stock. People bought tents and trailers and no longer needed guides or outfitters, and an empty Kineo House, which once seated 400 in its dining room, was a ghost resort.

Even so, Greenville still looks like an

Old friends catch up on the news at community breakfasts at local church.

outpost town. Float planes bank low over wood-frame houses that spill from steep side streets to the lake. There's a flushed, untidy, gritty feel to Greenville. It's had hard use and it shows.

More than in most places, Greenville's 2,000 inhabitants live here, not always for the usual reasons — jobs, money, family, and schools — but sometimes for reasons they themselves cannot explain.

I arrived in Greenville, Maine, on a Saturday in November, the first day of deer hunting season. It was a cold, gray afternoon with snow swirling against the windshield. I passed old farmhouses sheathed in plastic for the winter with clouds of smoke billowing from their chimneys. Men carrying rifles walked across bare fields that quickly turned white.

From the crest of Indian Hill just south of Greenville, Moosehead Lake (Maine's largest) appeared suddenly and dramatically through the snow, its islands covered with spruce. Mountains and forest stretched north, outlining the 40-mile lake. Greenville has long been the gateway to the north woods — 10,000 square miles of forest full of bear, coyote, moose, and deer that has been called "the last wilderness." Some say the wilderness is gone now that 2,000 miles of logging roads cut through it, but when the Army wants to train radio operators in survival tactics, it drops them into these woods.

In town, I ate at the Boom Chain, where the menu features steak and eggs, and daily specials like turkey, mashed potatoes, and gravy. Seven men came in, set two tables together, and sat down. Snow fell off their bright orange hats. One of the men was much older than the others. He walked slowly to the rest room, his hunting knife snug

Logging trucks rumble through the center of town, a constant reminder that Greenville's economy is tied to the surrounding woods.

against his belt. When he returned he ordered pie and coffee. "Good trackin' snow," he sighed, "but won't last until Monday."

They had arrived from Pennsylvania the night before. I asked what brought them to Greenville, since some of the best deer hunting in the country is in Pennsylvania.

The old man sipped his coffee. "Since I was a boy," he said, "it has been Moosehead Lake. Moosehead Lake. I had to see it. I worked whistle to whistle nearly 40 years. Always came here to hunt." He ate some pie. "I'm sick now, though," he said.

"You'll be hunting during my funeral," one of the men said. " 'Can't go,'

you'll say. 'Trackin' snow, too good to miss.' "

The old man laughed. "It's a shame," he said, "but you can't store hunting seasons. You only have so many."

I stayed a mile from the center of town at a modern and roomy place called Leisure Life Lodge. I fell asleep

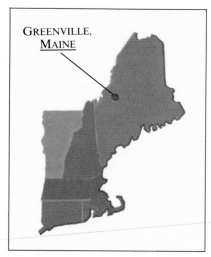

around midnight, but was awakened by a train whistle from the Junction across the lake. I stepped outside. In the glare of the lodge's lights I counted 13 deer strung to supports. Back inside, the windows were frosted and heat purred from the radiator. It was quiet and still — Sunday.

In the morning I had doughnuts and coffee in town at the soda fountain in Harris's Rexall Drugstore. The snow had stopped, and only a dusting remained on the ground. I bought the *Piscataquis* (County) *Observer* and the *Moosehead Messenger.* They were full of announcements for hunters' breakfasts and inducements for women to shop during "Deer Lonely Days."

I asked the woman behind the counter if she'd been busy. "Oh, they're coming in now," she said, "but we won't see them until they're on their way out. They just stock up and go to camps." I asked her how long she'd lived in Greenville.

"My husband and I drove up here from Rhode Island right after we were married," she said. "We got here at three in the morning. I'd been sleeping. I woke up and thought I'd come to the end of the earth. I said, 'Where's the town?' He said, 'You've just been through it.' I thought I would die. But you learn to like it. Anytime there's a tragedy everyone suffers. When someone prominent dies, we all close up. And when someone has good fortune, we're all happy."

The drugstore has been run by the Harris family in the same spot since 1896. As I talked with the woman be-

hind the counter, Ida Harris busied herself in the aisles. Her husband's father was the first druggist in Greenville, and now her son is the pharmacist. She joined us, and I asked if there was much trouble with so many guns around. She shook her head.

"The last murder was eight years ago," she said. "A woman shot a man while he slept in a sporting camp. There were three of us on the jury from here and we got her off. We figured she'd done the town a favor."

The man beside me at the counter began talking about the Indian woman who owned the basket store. She had collided with a moose the day before. "One time," he said, "a woman passed me going at least 75. She hit a moose. I got out and said serves you right. She got furious. I never go more than 35 around here. You don't want to tangle with a moose."

It was a short walk from the drugstore to the oldest and largest float plane operation on Moosehead Lake. Dick Folsom was born and raised in Greenville and by the late 1950s was flying more people over the north woods than all the other flight services combined. His pilots, including his son, Max, may take off 50 times on a busy day. Folsom is a wiry man with a soft voice and sandy gray hair. He squinted frequently, as though staring into the sun. He has had his share of rescues, and he used to bring supplies to several hermits.

"It's nothing like it was when I began. This used to be the end of the road. We had all the north country to ourselves. Roads are so good now, you can drive almost as fast as you can fly. People don't see the clearcuts and all the roads — but we see them flying over. I'll tell you the truth, sometimes when I fly over now, I could cry."

That afternoon I accompanied a weathered man named Al on a boat ride up the lake with a younger couple from southern Maine. They were interested in buying Allagash Camps, once a jewel among Moosehead's summer camps, to convert into sporting camps. Al, the longtime caretaker for the wealthy absentee owner, didn't relish the trip in the cold.

The camp was about 90 years old, well maintained, with two sturdy

Moosehead's productive waters drew sports and their money and a new way of life before the turn of the century.

docks, lovely grounds, and 36 cabins painted in creosote. Al struggled to match keys with doors. Inside one door we found a trunk full of rotting sports equipment. "I remember 50 years ago when Great Northern played the kids," Al said. "It was a big game and lots of people turned out."

The young man wore the cuffs to his jeans rolled up, smoked a pipe. His wife was snug in a snowmobile suit. They strolled quietly through each building, keeping their thoughts to themselves. There was an old wagon road, badly overgrown, and they figured they'd have to spend a bundle right off building a road two miles through the scrub to connect with a travel road. A plus was the spring that flowed off Burnt Jacket Mountain.

The man had worked for the railroad for 18 years. "They're laying people off," he said, "and they've put me on third shift. If you get a chance to work for yourself . . ." His voice trailed off.

Everybody got wet during the choppy ride back. The couple got out. "Well, we just have to go home and talk," the man said to the realtor who met them. "The thing is, can you make

a living here? Will it be a place you'd want to bring a woman to?"

Later that day I met 72-year-old Ed Lambert: trapper, constable, dog catcher. He drove up to the town hall in his red truck wearing a red shirt, red cap, and gray police trousers tucked into waterproof boots. His face was creased and gentle behind his glasses, his hair was gray, and he smoked a smudged black pipe that he tapped continuously with ruddy fingers covered with scabs.

"Want me to talk about the old days?" he said. "Makes me feel like an antique. I've been trapping 50 years. In the old days the old-timers wouldn't give you the time of day, but if they found something in your traps they'd kill it and hang it up for you so you'd find it. I've already lost two traps this year. Hunters going through steal them. We haven't had a hunting accident in many years," he said. "Maybe we need an accident or two."

He tugged a battered green notebook from his vest pocket and opened it. "Got nine fox, seven coon, three pine marten, one fisher, two mink." He paused. "And 21 rats [muskrats]. The wilderness is gone. My great-grandfather would tell me of his oxen who wouldn't move on some days — they smelled cougar. A man called the other

day. He wanted to come and trap foxes. 'Fine,' I said, 'bring a fox.'

"I put away a red tick pup today," he said sadly. "Hated to do it. If I were younger I'd have trained him on foxes. I hate to lay a dog away. I may as well spend my money on dog food. I'm too old to spend it on rum and women. What I like best is to go deep in the woods on a still night and listen for coyotes. I'll hit my siren and wait. I get all kinds of answers off the mountain."

On Tuesday at 5 A.M., sandwiches and thermoses of coffee were tucked into three trucks. There were five hunters: Jim from Texas, Tony from Georgia, Rainey and Leo from New Hampshire, and Harold from Maine. Their guide was Ron Masure, owner of Leisure Life Lodge, realtor, president of the Maine Guides Association, president of the Moosehead Wilderness Association, and a justice of the peace.

"I can marry you, sell you a house. Then if you get divorced, I can sell your house," he said. He came to Greenville in 1973, nearly broke. He had been a machinist, a baker, and a salesman. He was looking for a partner to build a resort — Leisure Life. He is 44, stocky, and talkative, except at five in the morning. "I've never been able to get out of bed early," he said, "except during deer season." He guides not for the

money, but because it allows him to be in the woods legally for three weeks. He grew up in small towns in northern Vermont, and his father bought him a Stevens .22 when he was ten. He ate so much venison as a boy that now he gives his away. His sports usually have success, and some say that Ron probably shoots several and lets his sports tag them. He denies it. "Sometimes I go with them and tell them when to shoot," he says.

We drove to Greenville Junction, then bounced along an abandoned railroad bed for several miles. It's harsh country for deer, but year after year the biggest deer in Maine are shot within 30 miles of Greenville. We stopped on a tote road. Three of the hunters chose to hunt along the road, while Ron and the others disappeared into the woods, each with a compass to find his way out. All morning and through the afternoon they stalked through bogs and thickets. Fresh deer signs steamed in the moss, but nobody fired a shot. By late afternoon the group decided to call it quits. Ron wanted to check one more place, a hardwood ridge on the side of a bog about a mile away. He drove up a tote road, parked, and entered the woods, walking only 50 yards or so before he stopped. A rustling, like someone shaking a branch, was coming di-

These hunters (far right) hired guide Ron Masure, in front of the group, to increase their chances of shooting a whitetail deer; on the average each season about one in three succeeds (right). Now there is a brief, hotly debated moose season, too (below), that means more hunters for Greenville.

agonally across the ridge. In the quiet you could hear a scraping of antlers against a tree. There was more crackling, more scraping, perhaps 70 yards distant. "Any man who kills a deer and says the kill isn't part of it, is a liar and a hypocrite and shouldn't take a gun into the woods," Ron had said earlier. Barely moving, he cradled his rifle toward the rustling. The scraping stopped, and Ron pursed his lips, cursing softly. "He knows something's wrong," he said. It was growing darker, and the only sound was the deer moving rapidly down the ridge.   *– November 1982*

Hartford, Connecticut

by Lary Bloom • Photographs by David Witbeck

ONE SPRING DAY LAST year, the fourth straight day of pounding rains, I opened my umbrella and walked toward downtown Hartford, through Bushnell Park, past the fountain trimmed in yellow tulips, past the State Capitol with the golden dome, past the Memorial Arch, past the bench where in dry weather I sometimes eat a cheese sandwich and a box of popcorn, past the path leading up to the statue of Lafayette and his horse. Somehow it didn't matter that I was getting wet. Or that for my first meeting with the mayor of Hartford I had wanted to look presentable.

No one, on this fourth straight day of miserable weather, could possibly be worried about fashion. The real concern was that the Connecticut River might overflow its banks, that Hartford might be threatened. In fact, I imagined that the mayor might be too busy supervising sandbagging operations to attend our scheduled lunch. But when I arrived only modestly soaked at Gaetano's, the lovely Italian restaurant, Mayor Thirman Milner was there, his fine and dry gray pinstriped suit belying the fact that he had already been out inspecting the critical sites. He was seated near the window, eager to talk about his town, where he had been born fifty years earlier. Indeed, he had been worried about the weather, he said, as the waiter delivered the bread. But there wasn't much that could be done. "We have better precautions now," he said, "not like the flood in the '30s. I remember that one. The Memo-

The architecture of the old Hartford is elegant in its detail (above) *and contrasts sharply* (right) *with the sleek new Hartford that's a-building.*

rial Arch was under water." I stared incredulously, thinking of that huge structure, drowned. "That's right," he assured me.

We were interrupted by the maître d'. "I'm sorry, Mr. Mayor, there is a phone call for you." Milner excused himself. As I waited, I looked out over Trumbull Street, at the most overpowering sights in downtown Hartford — the incredible collection of new concrete and glass office buildings. They are not much to look at in the way of design and architecture, but they are a strong sign of Hartford's economic vitality. It was hard to imagine that these monuments could be threatened by a river.

The mayor returned. "I'm afraid I'll have to cut the lunch short," he said. "The governor is about to call a state of emergency."

And so I ate alone and decided to be uncustomarily adventurous, ordering one of the house specialties, Pasta Calamari — a fancy way to say noodles and squid. Still, I soon found that instead of a culinary tour through Italy, this lunch was really an unexpected and imaginary walking tour through downtown Hartford. I tried to picture the Hartford that Thirman Milner once knew, juxtaposed against the city I have known for only four years, after having moved here from the South, and before that from the Midwest, where I was born.

And, in a way, I concluded that Thirman Milner's Hartford and my own were not very much different. Oh, yes, they were different in architecture — the buildings of old Hartford are almost without exception extraordinary in their detail and elegance; the buildings of the new Hartford are almost without exception extraordinary in their soullessness. Yet there is an odd blending of the old and the new, a healthy sense of business growth, and great regard for heritage and history. For me this tour of Hartford began to explain something I had not understood: why a place can make a nonnative, a non-Yankee, feel right at home after a lifetime of being a professional vagabond. As the tour unfolded — this imaginary and at the same time very real tour — the explanation became clearer.

I began this tour, surprisingly, at a

vacant lot. Well, that is, a lot that is now vacant but that will soon be a shopping center. Not a promising start, I admit. But, as with all else in Hartford, a little patience and understanding is required. About a year ago developer Richard Gordon proposed what he called a revitalization of the downtown shopping area. This revitalization, however, exacted some spiritual cost. To make way for the new complex, Gordon demolished the old Harvey and Lewis building, the city's last ex-

ample of art deco architecture. Gordon was roundly denounced by historic preservationists.

This brouhaha was notable, not because it demonstrated the trends in Hartford, but because it showed what *isn't* happening here. There are examples all over the city of the preservation of old Hartford life, from private homes to office buildings to "new" condominiums fashioned from ancient buildings; this is a real affection for the past, evidence that Hartford's heritage

is alive and well, and that this heritage becomes a part of our daily lives. It is the accommodation of the new and inevitable needs of the business community and the need for tradition and for roots that is at the core of Hartford's richness.

There are fine examples of places to live where the past is honored, most notably the old Linden, which has become the hottest condominium in town, a posh address on Main Street. It features high-ceilinged rooms and an

Bushnell Park, a 50-acre green in the center of the city.

Street vendors (above) *thrive in ethnic neighborhoods and history like Nathan Hale* (below left) *is kept alive, too.*

elegant restaurant, Spencer's. Congress Street, a whole neighborhood once given up to slums, is now one of the most desirable sections of town, due in part to the renovation of the buildings and in part to the persistence of its ethnic diversity.

But you don't have to live in town to understand and to become involved in its history. The great capitol debate is an example. There are those who prefer the old capitol, designed in 1792 by Charles Bulfinch, a tidy and handsome place that is the oldest extant capitol, or former capitol, in the country. When the new and much bigger capitol was built at the top of Bushnell Park, there was a public outcry. Many residents argued that the place was overly designed, too gargoyled. In fact, Hartfordites were ashamed of it. The story is typical. Anything new here is looked upon with great suspicion. The more I thought about this controversy, the more I understood about the nature of this place; there is absolutely no reason to dislike the new building — it is perhaps the most beautiful government edifice in the country. But it was new. It was different. And Hartford prefers anything to new and different — at least for a while. And when that while is over, it embraces the new with just as great a passion as the old.

Of course, if you spend a lot of time looking at City Place, you might conclude that Connecticut is a cold place to live. Two years old and 38 stories high, it replaced the Travelers Tower as the tallest building in the city, and is yet another example of modern downtown architecture. For some reason, critics bend over backwards to praise City Place, which is how you have to view it to like it. One resident calls it a "pink Formica monstrosity." One longtime resident gently describes it this way: "It is an awfully big elephant for such a small arena."

There is one fabulous modern structure. The Phoenix Mutual building, near the river, is arresting because of its elliptical shape, to the point where it has become known simply as the Boat Building. But, really, it is the little old treasures between those modern buildings, those places you can't see from the highway, that give Hartford its special personality.

171

Surely in that category is the Wadsworth Atheneum, the oldest art museum in continuous operation in the country, and one of the first buildings of distinction in Hartford, dating to 1842. The Wadsworth has a fine reputation for housing a strong permanent collection, and it was also once known as a champion of modern art. It, too, beckons those on Main Street to come in and browse, and to pass judgment on the two most controversial public sculptures in the city. The one in the courtyard is Alexander Calder's *Stegasaurus,* which, despite Calder's prominence in the art world, is considered by many observers to be distinctly ugly. In fact, when it was built in 1973, part of a memorial tribute to Alfred E. Burr, an owner of *The Hartford Times,* it met with great hostility. George Athanson, who was mayor at the time, said, "One day I see this thing going up. I don't mind being Calderized. But I don't want to be Stegasaurusized. Why was a two-ton dinosaur, known for its minuscule brain, chosen?"

Across the street from the Wadsworth Atheneum is an even more controversial work. The Hartford Foundation for Public Giving and The National Endowment for the Arts underwrote a minimalist sculpture by Carl Andre which is indeed minimalist; it is nothing more than an $87,000 collection of 36 boulders arranged in a triangle. At first I was outraged by the rocks. But now I kind of like them, although in this case I may be alone.

I'm not alone, however, in my appreciation of Lewis Street, restored as a Colonial showcase for modern law firms and restaurants; or for the Mark Twain and Harriet Beecher Stowe houses, resplendent in their detail; or the Marble Pillar, a real institution, a downtown Hartford chow hall, smoke-filled, gossip-filled, with a menu of hearty meals; or the nearby Italian neighborhood on Franklin Avenue, a genuinely friendly place in which to live or shop or develop an addiction to calzones; or for dozens of other places where, if you were to join me on a springtime walk, I would take you.

I would not take you, of course, to Constitution Plaza, an expensive lesson in the history of urban renewal, a project that displaced thousands of

Difference between old (above) *and new is shown clearly by 1871 Goodwin Building and City Place* (right).

residents in favor of new and cold offices. I would rather you see the positive side of Hartford because there is so much to see. The last stop might be the one you remember best, the one that might be the most inspiring.

St. Peter's Church on Main Street is an example of what makes Hartford's architecture, and the life around it, so interesting and integrated. St. Peter's,

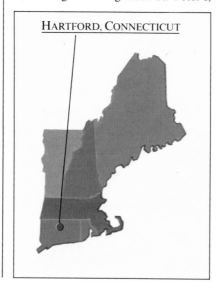

HARTFORD, CONNECTICUT

boasting the largest and perhaps most beautiful sanctuary in the state, was built in 1883, and was its most prominent and influential Catholic church — until the great suburban movement, when the executives flocked over the mountain to the west and to the rural communities east of the river.

A few years ago the church became so financially desperate that the sanctuary was roped off and closed down, and the sparse congregation, a few hundred lower-income families from the neighborhood, was left to pray in the church school. But when Father Michael Galasso arrived at his new parish, he saw the great possibilities. Patiently but passionately, he brought the church back to life; now, not only is the congregation praying once again in the main sanctuary, but people from all walks of life, and even from the eastern and western suburbs, are part of it. They proudly talk about how Father Galasso rummaged through the basement and came across a vagrant, one of the "street people," sleeping there for the night, and tried to wake him up — only it wasn't a vagrant but a statue of St. Patrick that had been relegated to the cellar for four decades. "It took eight men to get him upstairs," Father Galasso says. "We cleaned him up, and now he presides over the blessing of the shamrocks every March."

My tour was over, but the rain wasn't. I walked back through the park and thought about Hartford's image — not a particularly exciting one — and how that image discounted something very important. In some ways this town is provincial, in the worst sense of the word, but if you really get to know it, you can find no more comfortable city anywhere.

The park path led to Lafayette's statue, and I was reminded of a story told to me by Ellsworth Grant, the local historian. He said that when the statue was built, everyone approved of the likeness of Lafayette, and the horse was certainly a fine horse, but the neighbors to the south said they didn't want the horse's posterior to face in their direction. However, it was decided that Lafayette should face the north — toward the capitol. So the neighbors lost out in, uh, the end. Now they kind of like that view. And so do I.   *– April 1985*

Massachusetts

by Gunnar Hansen • Photographs by Jim Daniels

Island children gather for weekend play. After eighth grade, they go to school on the mainland during the week.

CUTTYHUNK ISLAND IS SIlent in the winter, except for the wind and the low, repeating rumble of the surf with the hiss of the withdrawing waters close after it. It snows little here, but when it does, the wind forms drifts against the houses, which are clustered near the harbor on the island's eastern end. Cuttyhunk is small — two and a half miles long and three-quarters of a mile wide — and the ocean wind blows across it almost constantly.

"It isn't the temperature down here; it's the windchill," says Hunter, an islander who claims no one knows his first name. In fact, Cuttyhunk stays about five degrees warmer than the mainland. "You get 15 degrees here," he says, "and the wind blows 30 to 70."

Even when the wind is relatively calm and the sea appears flat, the bell buoy to the south of the Neck, which forms the harbor entrance, rolls heavily from side to side.

The sea is gray-green, and Martha's Vineyard stands on the horizon eight miles to the southeast, a looming presence in the mist. When the air is clear, Gay Head and its lighthouse are easily

visible, and late in the day the flat winter light throws creases across its chalky yellow cliffs.

Directly to the east of the Neck, across Canapitsit Channel, lies Nashawena Island. Its tan grasses glow in this late light, shining almost gold, interrupted by patches of darker brush.

As I stand here on the hill above the village, starlings are gathering on the striped bass weathervane on the church below — a testament to the days when Cuttyhunkers guided bass fishermen.

Gladys Ashworth (above) *proudly displays her needlework at a weekly craft hour in the town hall, while Carol Monast shows off her newborn son* (left) *to neighbor Marilyn Lynch-Cornell.*

Today only a few persons fish or lobster (most of them work on the island's summer homes), yet the earlier islanders made their living from the sea, fishing and piloting whalers into New Bedford, 15 miles northeast across Buzzards Bay. In spite of their skills, the islanders of Cuttyhunk, the outermost of the Elizabeth Islands, witnessed many shipwrecks on the Sow and Pigs Reef to the west, and Hen and Chickens to the northwest at the entrance to the bay.

Many Cuttyhunk men were also

At 13, Duane Lynch is the oldest of the three children attending Cuttyhunk's one-room school.

CUTTYHUNK, MASSACHUSETTS

called upon to risk their lives at those times. When the *Aquatic* foundered on Sow and Pigs on February 24, 1893, six Cuttyhunk men went out in a boat to save its crew. Only one came back.

The West End is almost entirely wild, a mile and a half of moors, swamps, and ponds. Much of the landscape here is gray and blond and brown with splashes of red deciduous holly berries and bushes with clusters of indigo bayberries. The only signs of development clearly visible out here are a single

house and the windmill above the village on the island's highest hill. Built as a prototype generator to take advantage of the constant wind, the windmill never worked.

Now, in the fading light, no people walk down the village's main street; no vehicles move. The houses seem abandoned for the season. Then the wind carries the laughing voice of a man high on a scaffolding, working on a chimney — a surprising sound, reminding me there are people here.

About 35 or 40 persons live here in the winter. The exact number is hard to figure, since some come and go during part of the season. A few move off as they get older. Others, younger ones seeking a quiet life, arrive to take their place. Cuttyhunkers are peaceful and friendly, yet they want to be left to themselves.

The island, like all places, goes through its cycles of life and death. Late last January, Ray Cooper was accidentally killed on a West End beach

From the air, Cuttyhunk's small size, harbor, and windmill are easily seen.

when his pistol discharged. Ray was a quiet-voiced quahoger whose wife Ginger runs the island's only store. He was a man almost everyone liked, and his death saddened the entire island. This kind of loss seems harder to bear on Cuttyhunk than in other places, perhaps because the island is so small and because, though islanders stick to themselves, its isolation demands that everyone be concerned for everyone else on the island.

In the middle of this sadness, though, Cuttyhunk is also filled with life. Several young families have come to the island recently, and three children were born to islanders this past winter. "It's nice for an island," says Will Monast, whose son Calixte was born in January. "It's nice for the older people to see the babies coming." There are six children who will eventually study in the one-room school.

There are busier times. On Tuesday and Friday mornings Ellen Veeder, the postmistress, puts out the flag to let everyone know the mail boat from New Bedford is coming. These two days are also the only times people can get off the island unless they go by plane or private boat. Five minutes after the *Alert* has arrived, the post office's small lobby is filled with people pulling the mail out of their boxes as fast as Ellen can sort it. The post office is attached to her house, and the mail bags spill out into her living room.

Later, during the spring school break, the older children, who have

179

The windmill and the harbor
are testimony to the feel
of winters on Cuttyhunk
— a raw wind off a cold sea.

moved to schools on the mainland after the eighth grade here, will return. Then for a week the air will be filled with the voices of children.

But for now it is a Thursday evening in late December. As daylight fails, the inside lights come on in the houses. I see an occasional Christmas tree, or lights along a window, or red stockings hung against the window itself, glowing red as if by their own light.

This is the night of the Christmas party, a tradition for as long as anyone can remember. It is the one night of the year when all the islanders get together.

During the day Ellen has left a sign on the post office door: "I'll be back. If you need me, I'm up at the town hall getting ready for the party." She and Mary Sarmento, along with a number of others, have spent most of the day there.

Everyone on the island brings something. By 4:30, when the children begin to trim the tree, there are two tables entirely covered with food, for four tables of people. There's a lot of talk and joking as the dinner begins. It's more like a family, too small and personal to be formal or self-conscious. Everyone dresses comfortably in jeans, slacks, wool shirts, sweaters, and vests.

During dinner Frances Veeder, the senior islander everyone calls Gram, points out people to me and explains their family connections. Finally Gram says, "I still don't have some figured out." She moved onto the island in 1921.

After dinner the three schoolboys perform a skit about two city slickers at a country store. Then they shyly recite poems. Just as they finish, Santa Claus arrives with a heavy bag of presents to everyone's apparent surprise. The evening is filled with joy and applause and laughter.

Afterward I walk down to the harbor in the darkness. It's hard to think that this is southern New England, yet I can see the lights of New Bedford, and people sit in their living rooms here and watch television from Boston. Cuttyhunk seems so far away from all that, almost in a different time. The harbor is silent. The few boats at the dock lie still while the sea roars outside. I think of the name the Narragansett Indians gave this island: *Poocutohhunkunnoh,* point of departure.   *– December 1984*

Squam Lakes, New Hampshire

Mist rises from Little Squam
Lake at dawn in Ashland.

ON GOLDEN POND WAS filmed here," the woman says as she wraps the hand-painted loon figurine in tissue paper for the customer. "I watched them film the scene where Ethel had to take the boat under the bridge to the store. She was nervous, I could tell." The woman, who has her hair tied back in the style of Katharine Hepburn, stops a minute. "Oh, she was a beautiful lady. It was a wonderful summer. Now you know why we're loon crazy!" she adds as she hands the packaged loon to the man, who laughs and thanks her and walks out past displays of loon towels and loon T-shirts and loon ashtrays and into the parking lot, where loon whirligigs spin crazed wings in the breeze that's come up off Squam River, the only place anywhere near Squam Lake where there are stores.

On Golden Pond, which was filmed during the summer of 1980, had very

by Edie Clark • Photographs by Joe Devenney

little to do with Squam Lake's long-lived affection for this exquisitely shy northern lake bird. Long before movies were even dreamt of, there was Loon Island and Little Loon Island and Loon Reef in the midst of a lake where loon calls have trembled into the dawn and into the dusk for centuries.

Squam Lake could be called Loon Lake, or it could be called Golden Pond, but these are more modern descriptions for a lake to which the Abnaki Indians gave their word for water. Squam is the second-largest lake in New Hampshire, yet the passerby, driving along roads that dip and veer to-

ward the White Mountains, can catch only an occasional glimpse of this lake that's sprawled out like a spider over land so hilly it's no wonder the lake has so many islands. There are long islands and thin islands and round islands and tiny islands — all set in a lake so pure you can dip your cup into it and take a

During the filming of On Golden Pond *in 1980, both Caroline Nesbitt and Victoria James* (top) *worked as stand-ins. Local parents formed the Mom and Pop Band* (left) *for occasions like the Sandwich Fair* (above).

long drink. And along with those islands are reefs and coves and peninsulas and bays frequent enough that even longtime residents sometimes get turned around in the confusion of points and narrows that overlay the path from one end of the lake to the other.

"You get out here and you look around and you say, 'Where's home?' It's an easy lake to get lost on," admits Fred Rozelle, whose family has summered on Squam for 40 years, as we prowl down the narrows, staying in the channel marked out by red and black wooden buoys that stick up from the water like tomato stakes. Fred is president of the Squam Lakes Association

(SLA), which acts as a kind of surrogate town government for Squam Lake and its tiny sister, Little Squam Lake. The lakes are divided up into a confusing jurisdiction of five towns and three counties, yet those who live along the lakeshore do not belong to Sandwich or Ashland or Moultonboro or Holderness or Center Harbor as much as they belong to Squam. In essence, Fred is the mayor of Squam.

A sign with big letters requests "No Wake," and his flat-bottomed outboard slides through the water that's as black as long-brewed tea, past rocks that stand steady in the chop like silent reminders — Fred says that there's a boat on display at the marina with its hull bashed in, a victim of the rocks that lurk in the dark shallows. We pass into open water and speed up. "One thing that Squam does not have is large

expanses of water. It's shallow and cut up, which makes it less appealing to owners of big boats," Fred says, raising his voice over the buzz of the engine. Phil Preston, who is also along, is executive director of the SLA, and he remarks that the most appropriate boat for Squam Lake is a canoe. Fred agrees: "If you've got a big boat with a big keel, there isn't any way to get it onto the lake, short of dropping it in by helicop-

ter.'' Fred is a tall man who looks fold-
ed up in this minimal boat. ''Look at
that,'' he sweeps his hand across a
shoreline thick with hemlock and
birch. ''It's like virgin territory.''
Though there are no figures, Phil and
Fred estimate that there are maybe 500
cottages along the shore, but because it
has always been the tradition to build
camps that blend into the landscape,
the lake looks undeveloped.

We pass through a cove where two
identical-looking points of land face
each other. Phil, who says he's been
summering on Squam since before he
was born, gestures to the spot on the
left. ''That's where Katharine Hepburn
brought the picnic lunch when Norman and his grandson were out fishing.'' Fred looks it over and then turns
and sizes up the opposite shore. ''I hate
to disagree with you, Phil, but I think it

*View of Squam taken from Eagle Cliff
shows the relatively undeveloped look
of the sculpted shoreline.*

was over there — I remember seeing
the mountain in the background.''

Since there are few houses to serve as
landmarks at the lake edge, there is a
sameness about the landscape that has
provoked a lot of speculation and dis-
cussion among the lake dwellers: what

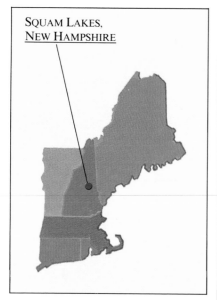

SQUAM LAKES,
NEW HAMPSHIRE

scene was filmed where. "I saw the movie twice, probably fewer times than the average person on Squam, but there were some areas I just couldn't recognize," Phil admits. Fred says he'd like to rent a video cassette of the movie: "It's better than seeing it at the movies, because you can stop action and really look at the background."

A loon and two chicks bob in the water ahead of us. Phil cuts the engine and trolls in their direction. The mother cranes her jet-black neck out of the water and cries in alarm. She curls into a dive and vanishes only to pop up soundlessly next to the boat, where she cries again, like a woman gone mad, until we reach a distance that suits her.

Farther on, Fred points to a spit of land. "There was a rumor that that was going to be sold to the Holiday Inn. Can you see it?" He throws his hands in several directions as if painting a picture. "Big towers jutting up. It would be enough to make you throw up." Earlier, Fred had told me that *On Golden Pond* had fit Squam. "The nature of the tale was really quite private. In the movie there was no evidence of any other activity except the mail boat. I guess they looked at a lot of other lakes in New Hampshire and in Maine, but for the purposes of filming, it would have been hard to capture that quiet at a busier lake."

Phil slows the boat and nods toward the shoreline, which seems like more of the same except for the flag flying from a boulder at the lake edge. "That's Rockywold-Deephaven," Fred says. "Over the years I'd say Rockywold has been the single most important influence on this lake."

Rockywold-Deephaven Camps is said to be the second-largest resort in New Hampshire, yet if you didn't know it was there you'd never find it, whether by car or by boat. And it is not what most people think of as a resort, but instead a kind of camp for adults, who come from all parts of the country — many of them for their umpteenth summer — to stay in small, rustic cottages that share a main dining hall. "For years the place was rigidly controlled," Fred explains. "You couldn't drink and there was a strict dress code. It was the kind of thing where if you didn't get a Christmas card from Mrs. Armstrong, it meant you weren't invited back."

The people who came to Rockywold shared an enthusiasm for simple living and a love of nature. They would have to, to want to travel that far (in the early 1900s, it took four days to get there from Philadelphia) in order to spend the summer away from their big, comfortable homes and live in camps that were sometimes no more than a tent, bathing in the lake, and reading by kerosene lantern.

Many of the families who first bought land on the lake had first been guests at Rockywold. They bought large tracts and have held onto the land, which has been handed down like the family silver, keeping the lake wild yet private. That wildness has continued to encourage wildlife to flourish — the herons and otters and beavers and, of course, the loons.

For each of the past 15 years, the residents of Squam have helped make a head count of their lake's loons. They were the first to make such a count, and this started a trend many other lakes have since followed. In addition, loon nesting areas are roped off in early summer, sometimes making as many as half a dozen islands or inlets off-limits to boaters or picnickers. On Squam, the loon population has remained constant over these last years of burgeoning lake use. This past year there were 44 loons and 12 chicks, just about maximum capacity for a lake this size. Neighboring Lake Winnipesaukee counted slightly fewer loons, though the lake is three times as big. Squam's success could be attributed to that abiding Rockywold philosophy of preservation.

Though it's a lake that many people would love to be a part of, Squam is a lake you can't have. Phil Preston points

out that there's a great deal of land on Squam that's never been up for sale. "There's no land for sale. Nothing's available for rent. Unless you live in one of the neighboring five towns, you can't swim there or even launch a boat."

"After *On Golden Pond* was made, there was a great flurry of interest in the lake. Real-estate agents were buried with requests," Fred explains. "There's a story that's probably apocryphal, but I heard that one of the real-estate agents here got a check in the mail for $200,000 with a note that said, 'Find me a place just like Ethel and Norman's.' Of course, he had nothing even close." — *November 1984*

At Piper Cove in Holderness, Squam presents a glimpse of its granite backbone. Formed in a hilly region, the lakes have myriad rocky inlets and islands that can confuse even the lake's most experienced boaters.

Caribou, Maine

The wind that swirls the snow in northern Aroostook County is like no other in Maine. People of the prairies would know it, for it is a farmer's wind, driving across the northern plateau into the valleys of the St. John and Aroostook rivers, unfettered by trees. Loggers came long ago to take the white pine and the spruce, and on their heels followed potato farmers who cleared the rest. From Houlton to Fort Kent, miles of potato fields stretch into the distance, their boundaries marked by thin stands of trees in place of stone walls.

A visitor's strongest impression of northern Aroostook is of distance — he cannot believe he can see so far. The land lies open on all sides, with horizons to match the ocean's. Perhaps it is the nakedness of the land, at once so utterly subdued by man yet so vulnerable to nature, that knits its people to it. For it can be argued that nowhere else is home and a sense of place more pronounced, more tenaciously guarded, or longer mourned when it is lost, than here in the Aroostook River Valley, which for its hub has Caribou, a city of 10,000, named for an animal last seen here in 1908.

Caribou is called the melting pot of Aroostook. Officially a city only since New Year's Day 1968, it is where the rich and varied ethnic lives of the region — the Scots and Irish, the Acadian French, the Swedes and the Lebanese — merge and blend like so many tributaries. And it is where the age-old family farm of 100 acres or less bucks up against agribusiness operations of several thousand acres.

Forty years ago Caribou was the largest shipper of potatoes in the world, a boom town with endless potential, but today there are serious problems here, as there are throughout the potato belt. Farmers are losing money, the land is losing its topsoil, the town is losing its

On a rise just off New Sweden Road in Caribou, a barn and windmill are silhouetted against a cold sunset.

by Mel Allen • Photographs by Stephen O. Muskie

young, and anger over the influx of Canadian potatoes threatens to explode into violence. Intermittent rumors rumble like thunderstorms that Loring Air Force Base, a prime civilian employer six miles east, will someday be closed.

But in Caribou people do not panic. Surviving hard times is bred into the children on the fields picking potatoes. The people are open and friendly, as gregarious a people as will be found in Maine, but made of more than a little steel cultivated through generations, able to weather almost any crisis.

And winter plays its part, tempering that steel. Stories of the cold — and of endurance — are passed down as heirlooms. Clara Piper, lifelong Caribou resident, recalls her parents talking about Friday the 13th of February 1861. "They called it 'Cold Friday,'" she said. "It was 36 below with a vicious wind, and it was unusual to have the wind with that cold. People who went out for just a few minutes had to struggle to make it back inside. But the mailman was determined to bring the mail. His name was Bubar, and he was known for his size and strength and appetite. He was always glad to be invited in for a meal. He went on snowshoes 12 miles to Presque Isle, got his load of mail, and started home. But the wind got him, and he cut down a cedar tree and kept a fire going all night to stay alive. The next day," she said proudly, "he brought the mail."

In 1939 the National Weather Service established its northeasternmost station in Caribou, lending authority to the old stories. With the exception of Mount Washington, it has the lowest daily mean temperature of reporting stations in the Northeast (38.8° Fahrenheit). Throughout the winter Caribou gains a certain national notoriety when, more often than not, it is reported to be the coldest town in the nation.

How cold? On February 1, 1955, Portland shivered at two below. That day Caribou set a record at 41 below, rising to a toasty 26 below the next day. Those are official temperatures. The weather station is located on Caribou's highest point, 600 feet above sea level, and amateur weather observers say that the cold air "drains" into the valley below, where it is at least ten degrees cold-

Since 1939 the National Weather Service has maintained a station in Caribou, here manned by Ray Glynn.

er on Main Street. Two years ago, the first five days of January told a chilling story: -9, -5, -24, -27, -20; still it was a mild month compared to the January of 1957, when the mean temperature was 1.3 degrees. But there is grudging affection for the cold and for the wind that creates whiteouts with the dry, drifting snow; there is mild scorn for people who surrender to the elements.

Two years ago, when the windchill

CARIBOU, MAINE

hovered around 100 below, a Caribou minister canceled his Sunday services for the first time. Some of his congregation were astounded and disappointed. They reasoned that there were storm windows in the church and ceiling fans to circulate the heat; anyone with any sense had plugged in his engine block heater, and the plows were clearing the drifts.

At 20 below the city is bathed in the frozen mist of warm, moist air rising from manholes. Water vapors from chimneys freeze across the valley and the blue silence of the Arctic descends. People walk the streets breathing through scarves, and twice a day they scan the sky for the weather balloons recording it all. At 100,000 feet the balloons burst, paper parachutes floating the instruments to land in a nearby field, it is hoped. Farmers are asked to return them, like hotel keys dropped in a city. Every hour the temperature is updated and the windchill noted, the better to advise schools and farmers, as well as the power company in case their men should be climbing poles that day. Firemen pace nervously, knowing that the combination of cold, dry air and overworked stoves could create a tinderbox should a fire begin and a wind arise.

Potatoes are shipped in winter, and farmers must take precautions that potatoes used to the 40-degree potato house are not ruined in a stiff northwest wind while being transported from barn to waiting truck. Even with care, cars sometimes won't start, and you would no more leave the house without jumper cables than you would without a coat.

Even so, the people of Caribou insist they'd rather see it 41 below in Caribou than ten above on the coast with all that moisture biting through. There are many people who insist that winter is their favorite time — the other seasons, they say, are laden with the anxieties of seeding and harvesting, and besides, it is so beautiful on those rolling hills covered with snow. Winter is when Aroostook catches its breath, the psychic conditioner for the laborious months ahead. When the people of Caribou have faced down another Aroostook winter, they know they can face the spring.　　　　　*– February 1983*

January has had a mean temperature as low as 1.3 degrees, so Jenny Richards is dressed for skating.

Hopedale, Massachusetts

THE STREETS READ LIKE promises: Peace Street, Union Street, Freedom Street, Hope Street, Progress Street. Hopedale is a town of about 4,000 people in southeastern Massachusetts, a bedroom community, and, though it's one of the youngest towns in the state, it has a rich history.

Hopedale was started in 1841 as a socialist utopian experiment, the creation of Adin Ballou, a philosopher who corresponded with Gandhi and Tolstoy. A branch of the Draper family, successful textile industrialists elsewhere in New England, set up a small mill in Hopedale. Ebenezer Draper admired Ballou and became a member of his idealistic farming community. But within 15 years the farm faltered and dispersed, and Ebenezer and his brothers were left to pay off Hopedale's debts.

By the river, at the tip of the pond, the Drapers expanded and built a new mill, a long brick building with almost as many windows as bricks. The mill

Philosopher Adin Ballou (above) put his utopian ideas to the test in Hopedale. Though they failed, Ballou is not forgotten. His statue dominates the town's park (right).

by Edie Clark • Photographs by Carole Allen

produced textile machinery, the Drapers' specialty. It covers more than 35 acres of the town's center, but, squat as it is, it takes a low profile to the rest of this unusually attractive mill town, the town that five generations of Drapers built.

The Drapers built a town hall, a school, a community center, and a gymnasium, and included extravagant touches like stained-glass windows and elaborate carved oak woodwork. They built a town library that looks like a miniature cathedral and made a park to honor Adin Ballou. In summer, they held band concerts on Wednesday nights and field days with races that offered cash prizes. In winter they kept the mill pond lit up at night for skating and a ski tow running on the hill at the edge of town. For the workers, they built spacious duplexes that step up from the mill, along streets lined with trees that the Drapers had planted as saplings.

Though the wages at the mill were low, the rent in the company houses was cheap — $3 a week back in the fifties, and that included heat and all repairs. Garbage was collected from

The Drapers, who were originally disciples of Ballou, carried on the community after its utopian experiment by making it a mill town. Their bustling mill complex *(below)*, **which produced textile machinery, was sold in 1967, then closed down completely and vacated in 1980** *(above)*.

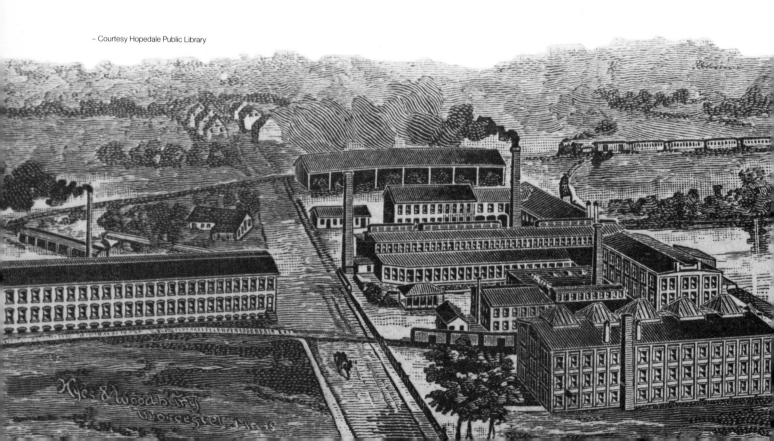

The Drapers provided attractive, varied housing *(above)* for their workers. William Gannett *(above right)*, who is the only Draper relative still living in Hopedale, stands in front of a portrait of great-great-grandfather Ira, who with Ebenezer *(right)* turned Hopedale into a flourishing town.

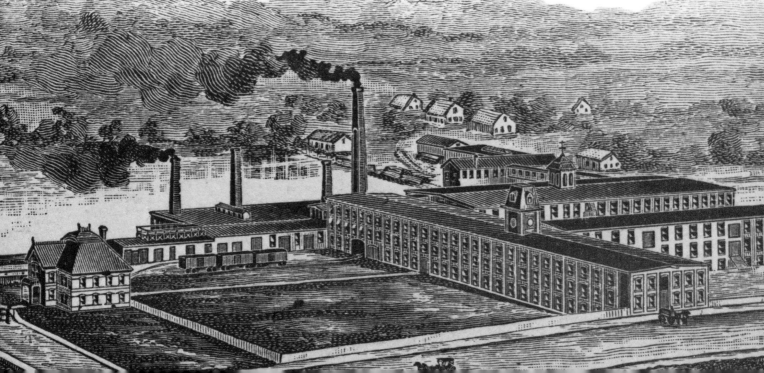

HOPEDALE,
MASSACHUSETTS

*Perhaps from an excess
of community pride, the
Drapers often built for the
town with ornate touches
like the marble statue*
(right) *in front of the town
library. Bea's Diner*
(below) *is a tenant in
Hopedale's town hall.*

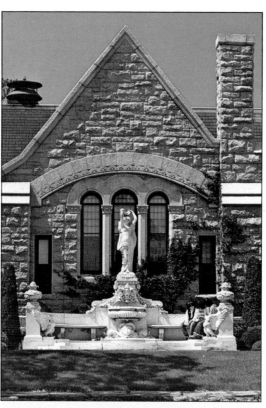

the back stoop. "Once a year they'd
come through and paint and paper a
room for us. They even kept us sup-
plied with light bulbs, but you had to
put those in yourself," recalls one longtime Hopedale resident. "When we
were kids, if we broke a window playing ball, the company would send
someone up to replace the glass." Another remembers: "We didn't have wel-
fare back then. It was the Drapers who
looked after us."

In spite of their wealth, the Drapers
were thought of as down-to-earth people who would walk through the plant
and know everyone by name. All

through those years when the mill flourished, there was everything that the streets' names promised. But, beginning in the sixties, the mill's business, affected by foreign competition, began to fall off. In 1967 the mill was sold to North American Rockwell, who, many people say, knew little about textile machinery, and in 1980 the mill closed its doors. Today it is an empty shell, looking for a buyer.

When Greg Burrill went away to school, his classmates nicknamed him Hopedale because he talked about it so much. He still does. "What brings people to Hopedale is knowing what it once was," he says. He has planned a condominium project to be built in Hopedale next spring, the first of its kind there. It's a project he hopes will bring growth back to Hopedale. The loss of the mill left a gaping hole in the tax base and, beyond that, there's a fervor among Greg and the town officials to keep Hopedale the kind of community it was when they were growing up.

In his office, 34-year-old Greg circles a portion of the map of Hopedale with his finger: "See how Draper developed the houses in clusters?" Greg moves over to where his blueprints are taped to the wall and circles a portion of the project: "We're going to build in clusters, too."

Down at Bea's, the diner that's part of Hopedale's town hall, there's a sign tacked to the wall behind the little boxes of breakfast cereal. It reads: "You can't get rich in a small town — there are too many people watching." Everyone in Hopedale watched the Drapers get rich, a wealth that in this case many say meant a better life for the town. It was paternalism with a gracious edge, the Drapers not unlike indulgent parents who wanted only what was best for their children.

– April 1982

199

by Tim Clark • Photographs by James Hyland

Thacher Island,

Massachusetts

With the abandoned north tower in the background, Harold "Whit" Whitaker raises "the easternmost flag on Cape Ann."

THACHER ISLAND WAS SETtled by accident 350 years ago, when a small boat carrying 23 passengers and crew was caught in a storm and smashed into kindling on the rocks. Only Anthony Thacher and his wife survived — their children drowned before their eyes. The General Court of Massachusetts gave the parents the island, 50 acres of rock and restitution.

In 1771 the government bought the island back and built twin lighthouses on it. Those wooden lights were replaced with 123-foot stone towers in 1861. Visible for many miles at sea, they guard the entrance to Rockport harbor and warn those approaching of the treacherous rocks of Cape Ann, granite fingers reaching hungrily for the unwary vessel.

There were times when as many as five families lived on Thacher Island, and there were enough children to make up a school. But the North Light was closed for economic reasons in 1932, and the South Light was automated in 1980 when the last Coast Guard crew left the island. Now the population is back to what it was in 1635 — one man and one woman, Harold and Sylvia Whitaker, the keepers of Thacher Island.

They are not there to run the lighthouse, although Harold, or "Whit" as most of his friends know him, keeps an eye on it and occasionally snaps a circuit breaker to save the Coast Guard a trip. They are there because, when the Coast Guard left, the Town of Rockport leased the island as a natural preserve and park, and somebody had to be there to discourage vandals, to keep the grass trimmed, and to greet and make welcome the hundreds of summer visitors.

Whit seemed destined to live on Thacher Island, though he never set foot on it before September of 1982.

201

Sylvia and Harold Whitaker
with their dog Mate *(left)*.
Only one of the twin lights still
operates *(below)*, and it's
fully automated. No longer is
there need for keepers like
Albert Giddings Hale *(below left)*,
who was here from 1861–64.

His mother was born there, and his grandfather, Albert Whitten, was a lighthouse keeper there from 1890 to 1900. He was perhaps the last man to see the doomed steamer *Portland* pass on the November night in 1898 when she went down with 200 souls, and he won a gold watch from the Canadian government for saving the crew of the

lumber schooner *Lottie B.* Whitten never saw the watch — U.S. citizens in those times were forbidden to accept gifts from foreign governments. It was awarded to his widow after the law was changed. But he found one of the ship's china serving platters miraculously unbroken on the rocks the next day, and it still graces the Whitakers' table on spe-

cial occasions.

Whit hasn't had to rescue any shipwrecked sailors in the two years he and Sylvia have lived on Thacher Island, but he plays an important role in protecting lives at sea. He makes daily weather and sea condition reports by radio, based on his own observations and reports from passing boats, and re-

202

cently the Department of Commerce gave him a Special Service Award "for helping improve weather service to the New England marine community."

Sylvia's contributions are no less significant, although so far unrecognized. She feeds the hungry Coast Guard helicopter crews when they drop in to make repairs on the lights. She pro-

vides homemade strawberry shortcake for the occasional visitor. She keeps the keeper's house, and keeps the keeper on his diet and on his best behavior. Perhaps she will be rewarded this June, on their 47th anniversary, if Whit succeeds in his avowed plan to get somebody to strike her a medal "for putting up with me."

If Whit wants it, somebody will probably do it. He has made hundreds of friends since moving to the island, most of them people he has never met. Their voices crackle over the radio with weather reports or messages to be relayed to wives on shore, greetings when the summer yachting season begins or farewells when the sleek boats head

THACHER ISLAND,
MASSACHUSETTS

south for winter moorings. They call on Christmas Eve from other light stations to report a fast-moving red light in the sky — surely Rudolph's beacon nose. Others sing carols over the static. The Whitakers are isolated but not alone. "If you have the stamina and the courage and the compatibility, it's a wonderful life," says Sylvia.

"There's something magic about an island," Whit agrees, going on to describe an evening when the rising moon silvered the ocean to the east of Thacher just as the setting sun turned the west to gold. They have even become so accustomed to the fog whistle that they hardly hear it, except to miss it when it stops. In T. S. Eliot's poem "The Dry Salvages" (a reef the Whitakers can see from their house), he speaks of "music heard so deeply/ That it is not heard at all, but you are the music/ While the music lasts."

Loblolly Cove is less than a mile away, but Sylvia has been ashore just three times in the last 13 months. A storm that tore away part of the dock, reducing possible landing times to four hours a day, is only partially responsible. The shore seems crowded and noisy to her now, their old house in Rockport hemmed in by others. She has bad dreams some nights when the wind shrieks past the keeper's house and the beacon light blinks in the windows. She dreams that she is marooned on the mainland and cannot get back to Thacher Island.   – *June 1985*

204

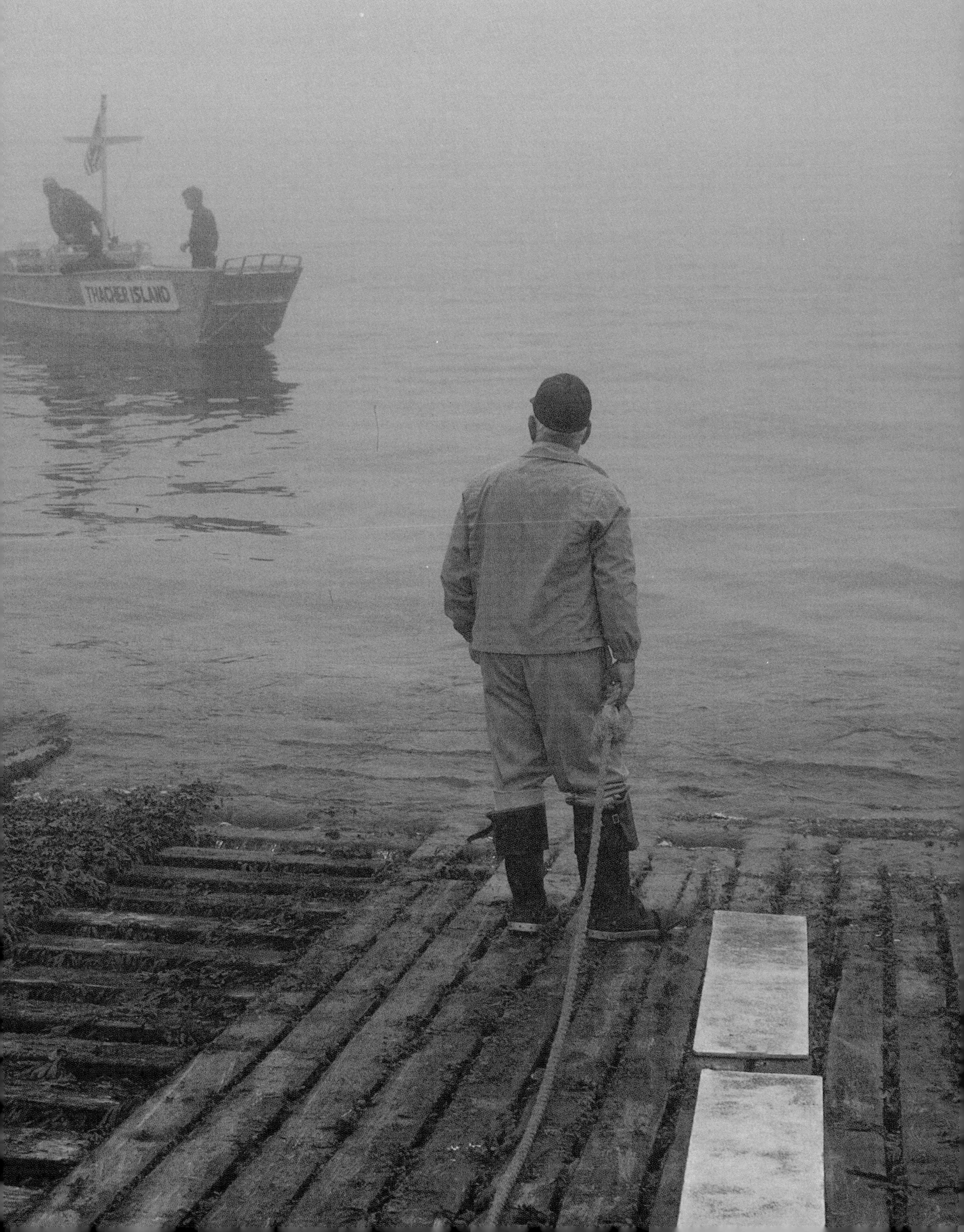
THACHER ISLAND

Nelson, New Hampshire

by Susan Mahnke • Photographs by Stephen O. Muskie

HILL FARMS DON'T pay." It's a line from a poem I heard long ago, and it might have been written for Nelson or for any one of hundreds of hill towns in northern New England, towns that had their heyday before the Civil War.

The highest hills in Nelson — Tolman, Fletcher, Osgood, Holt — stretch northeast from the village, part of the watershed that separates the Connecticut and Merrimack river valleys. The original settlers named those hills for themselves when they came in 1767. In 1775 Nelson boasted 186 residents. The population soared after the Revolution; by 1810, scarcely a generation later, the census counted 1,076 inhabitants, and Nelson was becoming one of the prime sheep-raising towns in New Hampshire.

But even as the hillsides were cleared of virgin stands of oak, chestnut, beech, and pine, and stone walls snaked over the highest ridges, the tide had begun to ebb in Nelson. The railroads made it cheaper to raise sheep in Wyoming and ship their fleece and flesh 2,000 miles east than to coax the beasts to maturity on the thin, rocky soil of upland pastures. It took no more than a generation or two to send ambitious farmers west in search of pastures literally greener — flatter, richer, not filled with glacial rubble. All the settlers left behind were their names on the hills.

As if to set their affairs — or perhaps their memories — in order, the 170 people left in Nelson in 1917, the town's sesquicentennial, published a history glorifying pioneer days, dedicated a monument to the memory of Nelson's Revolutionary War soldiers, and wondered with their poet, Ellen Taggard, "Where are the forms, the faces of yore?"

Nelson today looks much as it did in 1917. Nelson Village, not far from Center Pond, is approximately the geographical center of town. Around the common are the Congregational Church (thought to be a copy of a Bulfinch design), the 1787 Town Hall, the Old Brick Schoolhouse (now used for

Win French, town sexton, checks his mail and the pulse of village life.

Earl Barrett (top) *considers himself senior resident. Floppy Tolman and granddaughter Bee* (above) *manage a small flock of sheep. Win French stops his tractor to give farming advice to Michael Iselin* (left).

Ladies Aid meetings and town offices), the tiny Olivia Rodham Memorial Library, and a handful of 19th-century houses.

Town Hall, where voters meet the second Tuesday in March to talk about how much money the selectmen ought to spend, is alight every Monday night with the weekly contra dance. *The New Hampshire Times* recently called Nelson the contra dance capital of the world, thanks to the revival of the art by Ralph Page in the 1930s. That Nel-

209

son is the anything capital of the world would come as a great surprise to most of its residents.

There are 35 miles of state and town road in Nelson, but no railroad tracks. Nelsonians fought the railroads when they came as near as neighboring Harrisville, sensing correctly that their already struggling agricultural economy could never compete against the cheap labor and cheap land of the industrial age. What they hadn't realized was that the railroads that carried their children west would bring in a new commodity — summer people. The rugged landscape that defeated farmers invited city dwellers in search of that new element of the American dream, a vacation in the country. Around the turn of the century, Sadie Tolman, known to everyone as "Ma," opened her farmhouse on Tolman Pond to summer boarders.

Claire Partridge's family started coming to Tolman Pond in 1902, when Claire was just a baby. "We were the first ones to come," Claire said. "At

— Courtesy Nelson Bicentennial Album Committee

Each morning mail is delivered to these boxes (left) *in front of the Congregational Church, shown* (above) *when its steeple was repaired. Missy pulls Iselin children* (top).

first we stayed at the farmhouse with Sadie and Wayland, and then my father built a little camp that we called the Sugar House. It cost five dollars a week, including food." When Claire married Sidney Partridge of Boston, they in turn built a house near the pond and moved here permanently in 1958. Sidney served the town for 20 years as a

tax collector, earning a Lincolnesque reputation for fairness and tenacity. He once drove several miles over Nelson's notorious dirt roads to deliver a check for a three-cent overpayment.

As the 20th century progressed, other residents started to patch together a livelihood that included catering to summer people, caretaking the houses of those who went somewhere easier or smarter during the winter (there is a couple in town today who prefer to spend their winters in Alaska), cutting

cordwood, doing a little farming on the side, and, in many cases, indulging their artistic bent. Florence Tolman, known to everyone since childhood as Floppy, came here in the 1920s when she married Ma Tolman's son Fran, and did custom bookbinding. Fran was Nelson's moderator for many years and did sign painting and woodcuts. Albert Quigley, up in the Village, painted landscapes and portraits to barter for necessities. "And we had more people who could fiddle and flute than anywhere," Floppy said. "The whole town came to dances at Town Hall. At first the local people were ashamed to dance, but Ralph Page taught us. We hardly noticed the Depression — it passed us by with no great ups or downs. We just lived off the land."

One by one, the 11 original schoolhouses closed their doors until, by 1940, only two remained — one in the Village and one in Munsonville, a settlement on Granite Lake in the northwest corner of town — and they were in bad shape. Earl Barrett, who considers himself the town's senior resident ("Rodger Tolman is older," Earl explained, "but he left here to be a schoolteacher in Massachusetts for a while."), was on the school board in 1940, and he remembers saving the two schools from condemnation.

What building codes couldn't do, the waning population did, and in 1945 the brick schoolhouse on the common sent its eight grade-schoolers to Munsonville. Although the political and spiritual focus of town remained in the Village, much of the daily life of the town — school, post office, general store, the highway that led to Keene and Concord — was in Munsonville, crystallizing a split between the old landed gentry and what is perceived by them as the blue-collar commuters and newcomers. Floppy Tolman cautiously characterizes the situation as "stratified but not snobby, although some people assume it's snobby." Another Villager explained it this way: "Land seems to change hands so often in Munsonville."

The hill that looms over the Village to the east is, except for Mount Monadnock two towns over, the highest peak (2,233 feet) in this part of New Hampshire. The government's topographic map names it Osgood Hill, but local people always call it City Hill, a name that sounds ironic now, but was only proud hyperbole in more populous days. Settler Stephen Parker, the story goes, was plowing with his oxen on that hillside one June day in 1775 when a man on horseback told him that the British were menacing Colonial troops in Charlestown. Parker left his oxen in the furrow, went home to collect his musket and teenage son, and left to fight the battle of Bunker Hill. He returned to Nelson after the Revolution and died on the Fourth of July in 1814 after firing his musket 14 times, once for each original colony and once for George Washington.

George Washington never slept here, in fact never set foot here, but for years,

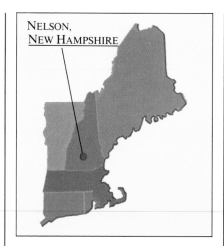

NELSON,
NEW HAMPSHIRE

reported Nelson historian Parke Hardy Struthers, his Aunt Mary Dane treasured a teacup from which she believed Washington had drunk on a visit to New England. It had never been washed, and privileged guests were allowed to taste the brownish ring around the rim and savor the hero's flavor.

In fact, no one terribly famous has ever lived here, and only a few of moderate renown. There was Alfred Beard Kittredge, born in 1861 on his parents' farm on Center Pond Road, one of many young men who left the town for the rockless soil of the prairies. He became a lawyer and then a U.S. Senator from South Dakota, and he drafted most of the important legislation concerning the Panama Canal. When he died, some of his belongings trickled back to Nelson and settled to the cellar of the library, where the trustees unearthed them last spring: a tarnished sword, photographs of white men and Indians standing together near a grove of trees on a flat plain, and, in a crumbling glassine envelope, three eagle claws taken from the dead body of Chief Sitting Bull.

Writer May Sarton lived here for a while in the late 1950s and early 1960s. She admired the strength and persnicketiness of the people, and wrote of them in several of her books.

There have never been lots of fancy houses in Nelson; it's not like neighboring Hancock with its main street of stately, impeccable, and unobtainable Colonials. There are no mansions, just farmhouses and cottages, usually in need of shoring up. This lack of grandeur has made Nelson accessible to

young people with families, and the town has experienced a population boom in recent years, back up to 450 people, about what it was in 1870 except that then the numbers were going down. At night, house lights flicker through trees on hills that have been dark for a century.

Just enough quirky, funny, exasperating, and sad things happen to keep life here interesting. Last year Newt Tolman, despondent after the death of his wife, sold development rights to hundreds of acres of Tolman land and used the money to buy a Rolls-Royce that can't negotiate the dirt roads. The town has had three different road agents in four years, a situation that has led to endless feuding and accusations. In the space of half an hour one April night in the town clerk's office, the newly defeated road agent accused his successor (in absentia, of course) of ruining the town equipment; he had no sooner left than the incumbent arrived to complain that the equipment had been left in such terrible condition that it already had to be fixed. When librarian Patty Packard's goats had twins and triplets last Easter, Reverend Carolyn Black announced it in church, right after the sermon.

Although less than two percent of Nelson's 15,168 acres is used for agriculture today, you can find sheep again in three or four pastures, and there is talk of pushing back the trees that have taken over the old fields, a task almost as backbreaking today as it was 200 years ago. People are starting to worry about zoning, and what kind of industry to encourage (if any), and what to do if someone wants to build a condo. As it always has, the land will determine the answers.

The hills of Nelson have dealt out defeat, and witnessed the flow and ebb and perhaps again the flow of a hill town. The people who stay here know they're lucky to have such poor and beautiful land, lucky to be afflicted with topophilia, a peculiar and incurable affection for a particular landscape. There's a spring in Nelson that people rely on during droughts when the dug wells go dry. Water flows into a stone trough upon which a farmer long ago carved the words, "My strength cometh from the hills."

– September 1985

**Chore time on the French Farm on
Center Pond Road brings Win and
his son Bud to feed the sheep.**

Sandwich, Massachusetts

THE PEOPLE OF SANDWICH
DEDICATE THIS MEMORIAL TO
THE SPIRIT AND SACRIFICES
OF 1776

by Bob Trebilcock • Photographs by Stephen O. Muskie

Every day, Jimmy McDonough feeds geese at the Thornton Burgess Society.

THE SUITOR OF SANDWICH has almost been forgotten. His story isn't written down, and how and where his life ended are a mystery. He was from a prominent Massachusetts family and lived before the turn of the century. He fell in love with Sally Pry. When she rejected him, the Suitor retreated to the woods to live like a hermit. Unable to possess the woman he loved, he carved her — he carved her form in a rock behind his house and he carved her in bas relief into his firewood. Hundreds of sexually explicit figures emerged, etched into his cordwood, and at night the Suitor filled his wheelbarrow with the statues and distributed them throughout the town as a reminder of his obsession.

Once, practically every boy in town kept a carving of Sally Pry hidden in the barn. The Suitor's family hired a man to dispose of these statues, and he heaved them far into the salt marsh that separates Sandwich from the sea. Despite the hired man's attempts to destroy them, the statuettes still surface now and then, preserved by luck against design. When the Cape Cod Canal was dug, nearly a cord of the Suitor's expression of failed passion was scooped out of the mud.

In August of 1987, when Sandwich celebrates its 350th anniversary, it's doubtful that anyone will commemorate the Suitor of Sandwich. Town eccentrics, like strange uncles, tend to be excluded from public functions. Instead, Sandwich will rejoice in its standing as the oldest town on Cape Cod.

Founded in 1637 and incorporated in 1639, Sandwich is presumed to have been named for a seaport in East Kent as opposed to the Earl of Sandwich. The Cape town was 118 years old when he was born. It is remembered as "the town that glass built," after the highly valued lead crystal produced at the Boston and Sandwich Glass Company from 1825 to 1888. Sandwich's most famous native son is Thornton W. Bur-

This photograph, copied at the Sandwich Historical Society, shows the work of the Suitor of Sandwich.

gess, the conservationist and author of children's classics, including the Peter Cottontail stories set in the old briar patch.

Both the glassworks and Burgess left their mark on Sandwich. The town historical society is housed in the Sandwich Glass Museum; 2,000 acres of land have been put under conservation, including an old briar patch that inspired Burgess's stories.

The sense of history imparted by the museums and antiques shops is very much a part of Sandwich Center's present. There are views from the historic districts of Main Street and the Old King's Highway that scarcely differ from the 1875 photograph that hangs in the selectmen's office.

Traveling along Route 6A from Bourne, Sandwich is announced by a hand-painted sign before the town comes into sight from across a salt marsh. The proximity of the village to salt water was a quirk of geography rather than a lasting influence: the pillared town hall, the tall spire of the "Christopher Wren" church, the shaded common, the abundance of capes and white Greek Revival houses, all combine to give Sandwich Center the manicured appearance of a 19th-century New England farming village. There are no neon signs, movie theaters, fast-food restaurants, or bowling alleys, and in fact it wasn't all that long ago that Sandwich *was* a New England farming village. Located on the northern shoulder of Cape Cod Bay, its beaches ringed by marsh, Sandwich was passed over by the first tide of Cape development in favor of warmer water and better beaches. As recently as 1960, the permanent population stood at 2,100.

But that was before developers touted a low tax base and proximity to Boston. With an estimated population of 11,589, Sandwich is the second-fastest-growing town on Cape Cod. The marina is the Cape's second-busiest port, and smokestacks from a power plant rise against the backdrop of a wilderness marsh while jets take off from a nearby air base. Like the statues of Sally Pry, new subdivisions keep popping up in unexpected places.

So much has changed in South and East Sandwich over the last 25 years that Carolyn Crowell bought a map to find her way around when she retired to Sandwich, her childhood home.

"People come here for the historical look of Sandwich," Carolyn said from her farm overlooking the bay. "But once they get here they expect city services and try to change the town. What I wonder is why they came here if they don't like it the way it is?"

As Sandwich prepares for its 350th anniversary, longtime residents lament the signs of expansion: a loss of wide open spaces has been accompanied by attempts to reorganize the form of town government and reform the church service. The utility company would like to replace the old incandescent street lamps with mercury vapor lights.

William Foster, a deputy sheriff and former police chief, grew up on a farm near the beach. Except for a brief stint in schools in Boston and in Providence, Foster has lived his entire life here in Sandwich.

"I left one fall and came home for good in the spring," Foster said. "That's enough experience to know that this is the place for me."

Now 70, William Foster is a sturdy man with broad shoulders, short white hair, and a firm grip. He and his wife, Mae, live at the end of Foster Lane, a dirt road lined with marsh grass. He has noted the transformation of his boyhood home from a close-knit community to a town of strangers.

"You take town meeting," Foster said from the kitchen where he drummed his fingertips on the tabletop while he spoke. "We'd have some humdingers for battles when I was police chief. But it wasn't personal. That's not true today. We just don't know each other. You take the people as individuals, they're the same. But collectively, the town has changed."

Change itself is something that seems to have come down through the ages. Sandwich was so fraught with development in 1858 that one writer of the day commented on the loss of wildlife in the area. "The town once proverbial for its rural pleasantries has been measurably shorn of many of its earlier charms," he wrote. Daniel Webster, a frequent visitor to the area, complained that the glassworkers had ruined his favorite fishing spots.

But the effect of the glassworks was limited to the years of employment. The glassblowers were an itinerant lot. Though the town boomed for several decades, between the closing of the factory and the current growth Sandwich's population dwindled by half. Life returned to a pace reminiscent of a Cur-

rier and Ives etching. In his autobiography, Thornton W. Burgess said of his formative years in Sandwich: "One can believe anything on the Cape, a blessed relief from the doubts and uncertainties of the present-day turmoil of the outer world."

Burgess was describing Sandwich at the turn of the century, when there were two drama societies, two weekly newspapers, a choral society, two bands, and two baseball clubs, according to the town history, *Sandwich: A Cape Cod Town.*

It was a time Rosanna Cullity remembers well. Rosanna represents the ninth generation descended from Benjamin Nye, one of the town's original 50 founders. When she was a girl in the 1920s, her brother owned a skeleton of a Model T. The children could drive from Sandwich to West Barnstable without crossing a paved road. On Saturday nights, the town danced in the Grange Hall to piano and fiddle music or played whist.

"I can still remember when the electricity was installed," Rosanna said. "We would visit each others' homes

just to look at a light bulb. Isn't it sad to sound so dated?"

"To outsiders, this is still paradise," Walter Cullity commented. "But we remember these things. And when we see these changes, it upsets us."

Mornings are quiet along Main St. (above), but deputy sheriff William Foster (left), a lifelong Sandwich resident, notes changes in the town.

In 1959, when the State of Massachusetts wanted to tear down the old Nye Family Homestead, Rosanna sent letters around the country to 2,500 Nye family descendants and asked for support to save the old house. Today, it is a 17th-century showplace where the family gathers every other year for a reunion.

"These are my roots," Rosanna said. "I love history, and I love the town. To see an old house torn down is like watching a ship sinking in the ocean."

When William Foster thinks about his boyhood in Sandwich, he remembers hunting in the thickets with his father. Now he says he wouldn't fire a gun into the woods for fear of hitting a subdivision.

His father grew cranberries and raised livestock on a farm close enough to the beach to smell the sulfur of the marsh and the ocean salt. In the winter, he cut ice from the ponds. It was called

"chocolate ice" because of the brown pond water.

Foster also recalls when the first summer house went up on Spring Hill Beach in the 1920s. The lane to the shore passed through his father's pasture. The summer people had to close the gate behind them so the cows didn't get out. The new arrivals purchased eggs and milk, a boon to the Foster farm. But they also changed the ice business.

"Most people around here used ice just to preserve their food," Foster said. "But the summer people wanted ice for their drinks. They objected to Dad's chocolate ice, and he had to find a clear pond the next winter."

THE DISTINCTION OF BEING THE oldest town on the Cape is worth shouting about. Throughout the years, Sandwich has always been more than willing to strike up the band and form a parade to celebrate just about anything.

The 250th anniversary was the largest event on the Cape of its day. The Grand Parade included five bands, a cavalcade of 75 horsemen, Masons galore, military guards, and invited guests in carriages. A chorus of 50 sang the "Gloria" from Mozart's 12th Mass while a Venetian carnival of 40 boats

Rosanna Cullity (above) showed her pride in her family home, the Nye Homestead, by rallying family members from far and wide to save the home from demolition in 1959. As this house on Grove St. (left) shows, Mrs. Cullity is not alone in her pride.

Sunrise at Springhill Beach in East Sandwich catches a motor boat at rest before work begins.

MS 1

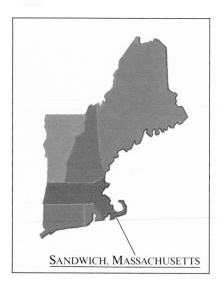

SANDWICH, MASSACHUSETTS

*Sarah and Lauren Goodman pause on
the footbridge leading to Town Beach.*

decorated with Japanese lanterns floated on Shawme Lake. The clambake
was attended by 2,000.

Since then, Sandwich has celebrated
the 275th, 300th, and 325th anniversa-
ries. Back in 1964, William Foster was
directing traffic when two candidates
for governor arrived separately by helicopter to share in the 325th celebra-
tion. The pair of politicians posed for
photographs next to three girls on
horseback.

"That's the first time in my life I saw
three horses' heads and five horses'
asses," Foster said.

The organizers of the 350th anniversary have planned a ten-day celebra-
tion that's unrivaled in Cape history,
including two clambakes, six concerts,
fireworks displays, a historical play,
and the largest parade ever held on the
Cape. The planners see it as a day not
only to celebrate the past, but to ac-
knowledge the new influences shaping
the future of the oldest town on Cape
Cod. Rosanna and Walter Cullity plan
to be there.

"I think all Yankees are pretty proud
of their heritage," Walter said.

"With all the changes," added Rosanna, "it's still the most beautiful
town I know of."

William Foster isn't sure if political
candidates will again arrive by helicopter, but he expects big things.

"It'll be a humdinger," he assured,
and rapped his knuckles on the kitchen
table for good luck. "A real lollapa-
looza."   *– August 1986*